MADE AT HOME
CHEESE & DAIRY

For Angela – D.S.
To Holly – J.S.

Cheese & Dairy
by Dick & James Strawbridge

First published in Great Britain in 2013
by Mitchell Beazley, an imprint of
Octopus Publishing Group Limited,
Endeavour House, 189 Shaftesbury Avenue,
London, WC2H 8JY
www.octopusbooks.co.uk

An Hachette UK Company
www.hachette.co.uk

ISBN: 978-1-84533-753-7

A CIP catalogue record for this book is
available from the British Library

Printed and bound in China

Neither the authors nor the publishers take
any responsibility for any injury or damage
resulting from the use of techniques shown or
described in this book.

Both metric and imperial measurements are given
for the recipes. Use one set of measures only,
not a mixture of both.

Standard level spoon measurements are used in
all recipes
1 tablespoon = 15ml
1 teaspoon = 5ml

Ovens should be preheated to the specified
temperature. If using a fan-assisted oven,
follow the manufacturer's instructions for
adjusting the time and temperature. Grills
should also be preheated.

This book includes dishes made with nuts and
nut derivatives. It is advisable for those
with known allergic reactions to nuts and nut
derivatives and those who may be potentially
vulnerable to these allergies, such as pregnant
and nursing mothers, invalids, the elderly,
babies and children, to avoid dishes made with
nuts and nut oils.

It is also prudent to check the labels of
preprepared ingredients for the possible
inclusion of nut derivatives.

The Department of Health advises that eggs
should not be consumed raw. This book contains
some dishes made with raw or lightly cooked
eggs. It is prudent for more vulnerable
people, such as pregnant and nursing mothers,
invalids, the elderly, babies and young
children, to avoid uncooked or lightly cooked
dishes made with eggs.

MADE AT HOME
DICK & JAMES STRAWBRIDGE

CHEESE & DAIRY

MITCHELL BEAZLEY

CONTENTS

INTRODUCTION

Dairy products make up an important part of our diet, yet most people rarely think about where they come from or how they are made. Traditionally, people made their own cheese according to local methods or family recipes passed down the generations. Home cooks would take pride in their regional variations and the individual character of the dairy produce they made. Fortunately, there is currently a renaissance within the food industry with small-scale businesses and artisan cheese-makers gaining popularity and making reputations for themselves. The dairy industry is once again being creatively shaped by passionate people.

HUMBLE BEGINNINGS

All dairy products stem from one ingredient and there are hundreds of different ways to use it. Milk is fantastic: it is full of flavour and very nutritious. Buying fresh local milk not only supports the local economy but also gives you the most amazing ingredient to play with. You don't need a dairy or a cow to enjoy making cheese, butter or yoghurt. You don't even need a farmhouse kitchen and specialist equipment -- all you need is milk!

Gone are the days when a family would have their own cow and milk her daily as part of the household chores. Most of us now leave this to farmers and commercial dairies. If you have the space and time on a smallholding or farmstead, we're sure that it would be even more satisfying to try the recipes and techniques in this book with your own milk. But for the rest of us it is all about enjoying the control of a process from simple beginnings to a special product. Try to buy your milk from a local producer, the fresher the better. Try goats' and ewes' milk if you can find it, and remember that all the products in the dairy aisle at the supermarket can be made at home from this simplest of ingredients.

START SIMPLE

If you want to pick up this book and make a blue cheese with no prior experience then good luck to you! However, we'd strongly suggest starting with some of the more basic methods before progressing into the world of complex cheese-making. We started years ago with simple yoghurt recipes and butter-making and have gradually built up our confidence and experience. If you have the chance to visit a local artisan cheese-maker or shop, ask questions about the process. Moreover, take notes on your own experiences and attempts so that if you have a problem you can look back and see where you went wrong.

The beauty of cheese-making and producing delicious dairy products is that it is a meticulous skill. The methods have evolved over thousands of years, sometimes by mistake, but always with reflection and careful practice. Not everything in this book will work first time for you but the majority of your attempts will leave you beaming. Enjoy perfecting the simpler recipes and, when you understand the principles, start experimenting with various levels of acidity, time and flavourings.

We have learnt that working with milk is remarkably scientific. The reason we love making our own dairy products is that the alchemy of transforming milk into rich clotted cream or fresh butter relies on some relatively simple laws of science. Once you feel that you understand the basic processes of coagulation, making cheese and other dairy products becomes as straightforward as baking bread.

TAKE CONTROL OF YOUR FOOD

Making your own yoghurt, butter and cheese not only saves money but also means that you know what you are eating. You may not know the name of the cow or goat that supplied the milk, but you can be sure that everything you serve is under your control. This is part of the reason we are motivated to wait in the kitchen late at night testing the curds and whey, adjust the temperature of a batch of soured cream first thing in the morning and generally pay such close attention to our dairy. For us there is a transparency about buying such inherently simple ingredients as milk or cream, then using them to build up into more complicated food.

CREATE SOMETHING UNIQUE

The other major attraction behind making cheese and dairy is pride. We love eating and sharing a food that we've made at home. We also love creating something unique: if you try any of these recipes, not one single batch of yoghurt, cheese or butter will taste the same as ours. The aim is to make something similar, but the excellent thing is that the subtle differences are what we celebrate. The local humidity, climate and environment will affect your starter cultures, the weather will affect the grass that the cows eat and thus the taste of the milk, and even your kitchen will impress its own stamp on the taste of your cheese. If you want to enjoy eating something special and unique, sterilize some equipment and buy some milk -- your Made at Home dairy is waiting for you!

PREPARING THE

DAIRY

In the past, many large homes had a dairy room or buttery that was reserved for the activities described in this book. Nowadays we have lost most of these specifically allocated rooms, but on the whole our homes are well suited to making cheese and dairy products with good insulation and clean surfaces. If you want to succeed in making delicious dairy produce from your home you will need to adjust your kitchen so that it is clean, ordered and possesses suitable conditions for the delicate growth of beneficial bacteria. It is very quick and simple to adapt your kitchen into a home dairy.

GET ORGANIZED

Start by removing as much clutter as possible from work surfaces and then properly clean the area. The aim when making many dairy products is to create the perfect environment for beneficial bacteria to grow and transform the milk, so you need to make sure that the only bacteria around are those you introduce yourself in the form of a culture. If you want windows open for ventilation, it could be worth putting up some fly screens so that you don't get insects in your milk.

The starting point to consider before making any cheese or dairy goods in your kitchen is the space itself and the different areas that you will need. Ideally, if you are making cheese, you need to lay out three sections – production space, drying space and ageing space.

PRODUCTION SPACE

For the production of cheese or yoghurt you will need the hob and a clean surface near to it. This part of the process benefits from an ambient room temperature of around 21–25°C (70–77°F). First the milk is curdled by adding rennet and a starter so the space should be light and easy to work in for exact measuring out of ingredients.

The next process is usually draining; we tend to clear the sink and draining board for this. You will probably need space for some large plastic buckets or pans to capture the whey and also racks and cheese mats to allow drips to escape without messy pooling. Then comes pressing, shaping or moulding, which requires its own clean surface. This may sound like a lot of space but we have managed in very small kitchens.

DRYING SPACE

This stage involves drying the cheese and removing any remaining whey and surface moisture. The temperature should be 12–21°C (54–70°F) and good ventilation is crucial. Try to use a room on the north-facing side of the house, or use an electric fan to improve ventilation.

AGEING SPACE

Some cheese needs to be aged before it is enjoyed and this requires a lower temperature of around 5–10°C (41–50°F). A cool cupboard, pantry or refrigerator may be the ideal spot. Alternatively, make a ripening box (see page 75) and move it to the coolest part of your home.

BASIC EQUIPMENT

It is essential to measure the temperature of the milk during many of the processes described in this book, so you will need a thermometer. There are clip-on dairy thermometers that fit on the edge of the pan, floating thermometers and digital thermometers, but choose something simple and easy to read. The benefit of digital thermometers is that the reading is almost instant, so they remove some of the room for error. Use whatever you have to hand and don't forget you will also have to monitor the room temperature when drying and ageing cheeses.

Perhaps the most useful item in the dairy is the humble jam jar. A glass jar with a sealable lid will be handy for many parts of the dairy process and can be reused countless times. Sterilize them well each time you use them and replace the rubber seals on kilner jars every few months.

There are all sorts of retro tools and pieces of equipment that are still very practical today. We have collected churns, moulds and presses over the years and find that they are easy to clean up and use again.

EQUIPMENT FOR HEATING MILK & CREAM

Most of the techniques in this book require the milk or cream to be heated. In some cases it can be heated directly in a pan over a gentle heat. In other cases, the milk or cream has to be heated very gently over a period of time, then kept at a constant temperature. For this, indirect heat is required, and this can be provided in one of three ways.

The most low-tech approach is a water bath. A large preserving pan or other wide pan is ideal for this. The milk or cream is poured into jars or other containers and they are placed in the large pan. The pan is then filled with water to halfway up the sides of the jars or containers. Place the pan over a very low heat to increase the water temperature very slowly. You can quickly adjust the water temperature by adding some cold water if necessary. When monitoring your progress, remember to measure the temperature of the milk or cream, not the surrounding water.

The second option is a double boiler. This is a large pan, which is filled with water and heated on the hob. A receptacle sits on top of the pan, holding the milk or

cream, which is warmed from the gentle heat rising from the water below.

The third option is an electric soup kettle. This appliance is basically a metal jacket containing warm water which surrounds a pan, into which is poured the milk and cream. The unit is thermostatically controlled and makes the whole process very easy as you can set it to whatever temperature you like. If you are serious about making dairy produce, this is a good investment. Soup kettles are not very expensive and can be used for most of the techniques in this book.

CLEANING & STERILIZING

Cleanliness in the dairy is vital. Before you begin any of the techniques in this book, wash your hands thoroughly. Avoid wearing perfume or fragrances as these will instantly taint your cheese, and refrain from cooking other foods while making cheese as this will not only distract your attention but also risk cross-contamination.

Keep your kitchen work surface clear from clutter so that it is easy to wipe down. We use a solution of 2 tablespoons of bleach to 4.5 litres (1 gallon) of water for general cleaning. It is a good idea to sterilize the sink before you begin. We use sterilizing granules, of the type used in home-brewing, dissolved in boiling water. Fill the sink with the sterilizing solution, leave for 15–20 minutes, then empty it and rinse well.

It is also vital to sterilize all your utensils, moulds and equipment before you begin. These can be soaked in the sterilizing

solution in the sink, then rinsed well in hot water before use. This final rinse is very important as anti-bacterial cleaners are not selective and will kill your beneficial bacteria too. After use, rinse dirty equipment with cold water first, rather than hot. The dairy curds will often stick to a surface when heated rather than flowing down the sink.

USING STARTER CULTURES

Many dairy products are made using a bacterial culture to sour the milk or cream. These are readily available online from specialist cheese-making suppliers, and there are different starters for creating different things, whether it is blue cheese or soured cream.

These freeze-dried starters should be stored in the refrigerator, then brought to room temperature an hour before you intend to use them. Different starters operate best at different temperatures, so a water bath and thermometer are essential to ensure you are giving the starter a chance to develop. For example, the optimum temperature for a mesophilic starter culture to develop is 30°C (86°F) but it will work between 20–38°C (68–100°F).

The best method to activate a starter is to sprinkle it over the surface of the milk or cream when it has reached the correct temperature. Leave the starter on the surface for 5 minutes to rehydrate. Next, use a sterilized whisk to gently stroke the starter up and down into the liquid so that it is incorporated from the top to the bottom. This, rather than just stirring in circles, will help the curds form more evenly throughout the milk or cream. As a rough guide, try to stir it gently at least 20 times before leaving the culture to develop.

RENNET & CALCIUM CHLORIDE

These two ingredients are needed in some dairy techniques, and both are readily available from cheese-making suppliers. Rennet is an enzyme derived from cows' intestines, which solidifies proteins in the milk to form curds. We use a liquid rennet, which has to be diluted in sterilized water before it is added to the milk. Avoid chlorinated water as it can kill the enzyme. Bottles of rennet will last for a few months in the refrigerator and are available in vegetarian form. Lemon juice is sometimes used instead of rennet as it also coagulates the milk, but it works at higher temperatures.

Calcium chloride is used in the making of some cheeses to help firm up the curds as they coagulate and replace the calcium removed during the commercial pasteurization and homogenization processes.

REALISTIC PLANNING

It is tempting to dive in and make huge quantities with your new gadgets and know-how, so put in some thought and planning before you start. Try to resist the temptation of mass-production and make small batches more often. This will provide you with a lovely variety of products in your refrigerator from which to choose. Work with your available space and plan ahead, knowing that some types of dairy need time to age and mature before you can eat them.

1

MILK & CREAM

INTRODUCTION TO

MILK & CREAM

Milk is a key part of our diet from birth. Mammals developed milk to raise young, but man has been milking domesticated animals and creating dairy products since recorded history began. Milk is essential for babies and children to aid good bone and brain development, and there are great health benefits for adults too. All the milk we use is conveniently shop-bought and doesn't rely on our almost non-existent milking skills -- there are unhappy cows in dairy farms all around the country where we have tried milking with no great success! Most of the milk we buy is pasteurized and homogenized because that is how it is usually sold.

TYPES OF MILK

Milk has a complex structure that allows it to change into the dairy products that we know and love. The proteins help with coagulation, the sugars turn to acids under the right conditions and the globules of fat provide the unbeatable taste. In the past people would have milked mares, camels and buffalo, but most countries have now adopted the cow for their commercial milk demands. We love the taste of cows' milk but also use goats' milk regularly. Ewes' milk is also delicious and is used to make some of the cheeses in this book, but it is more difficult for us to source locally.

COWS' MILK

The colour of cows' milk tends towards creamy-yellow and this is due to the carotene in the grass they eat. Certain breeds will produce milk that is a paler or a deeper yellow and the subtle taste of the milk will vary according to the season and the cows' diet. Cows' milk is lovely to use for cheese-making and readily available. It contains around 3–3.5 per cent fat and 3 per cent protein.

GOATS' MILK

Unlike cows' milk, the milk from a goat is very white. The acidity of goats' milk is higher than that of cows' milk, which explains the gentle tang and citrus quality you get when tasting it. This acidity also makes the fat particles smaller and the curds finer when it is used to make cheese and yoghurt, thus it is easier to digest. Goats' milk contains around 4 per cent fat and 3 per cent protein.

EWES' MILK

This is slightly harder to find but worth searching for! Ewes' milk also lacks the colour from carotene but it is superb for making cheese and yoghurt as the level of both protein and fat is high. It has around 8 per cent fat and 5.5 per cent protein.

BUFFALO MILK

If you have a local source of buffalo milk, it can be used in many of the recipes later in the book, most notably for making mozzarella (see pages 116–7). Buffalo milk contains around 6 per cent fat and 4.5 per cent protein and is wonderful for cheese-making.

Goats' milk is much whiter and tangier than cows' milk

BUYING MILK

Buy fresh local milk wherever you can. Pasteurization allows milk to be transported further, but for the best quality you should try to buy it close to home. We are fortunate to be surrounded by herds of dairy cows and our local farmers swear that the good grass produces great milk.

The other benefit to buying locally is that you can ask the producer about the milk. If cows have been treated with antibiotics, the residues in the milk can affect live cultures and interfere with cheese- and yoghurt-making. If you buy milk direct, you can ask if the milk is suitable for use with live cultures and ascertain how recently the cows were treated.

RAW MILK

Raw milk comes straight from the udder and is not treated. It contains more natural bacteria and is favoured by artisan cheese-makers because the flavour can be more complex and it curdles more easily. Many cheese-makers maintain that any potentially harmful bacteria are killed if the cheese is ripened for 60 days or more. However, for the safety of pregnant women and young children in our family we prefer to use treated milk.

PASTEURIZED MILK

Pasteurized milk is the standard in most areas. We have met ardent supporters of raw milk who believe that pasteurization is damaging to the internal balance of our bodies and our immunity. We believe that there are other ways to consume beneficial cultures of bacteria to aid our digestive systems without risking illness from unknown herds of cows. Therefore, we always buy pasteurized milk because if it is stored properly we know it is safe.

To pasteurize raw milk at home, heat the milk over a period of 30 minutes using a water bath or double boiler (see page 12) until the temperature reaches 66°C (151°F). Cover and retain at this temperature for another 30 minutes. Plunge the container of milk into an ice bath for 30 minutes to cool it quickly to 4°C (39°F), then refrigerate until ready to use.

HOMOGENIZED MILK

Homogenized milk is the result of a mechanical process which breaks down the fat particles in the milk so that they can't rise to the surface and separate into cream. It is therefore not as good for making butter and cream, but excellent for freezing. Most of the milk available in large supermarkets is both pasteurized and homogenized.

SKIMMED, SEMI-SKIMMED & WHOLE MILK

Milk is available as whole, skimmed or semi-skimmed and the difference between the three is in the fat content. Whole milk, straight from the cow, contains 3–3.5 per cent fat, semi-skimmed milk contains 1–2 per cent fat, while skimmed milk has had all of the fat removed. The fat content of whole milk does vary, depending on the breed of cow, the cow's diet and the time of year.

CREAM

Cream is the ambrosia of the dairy world. It is thick and surprisingly or not, creamy. We love the way you can use cream in so many different ways. It can be cultured and transformed into soured cream or crème fraîche, or heated to develop a crust and become clotted cream. You can cook with it or freeze it and it takes on flavours like a bus picking up passengers.

Finding really delicious cream depends on where you live but it is worth looking for a supplier that offers rich, deeply flavoured cream. We tend to buy cream already separated from the milk because it saves time and leaves us with less waste. If you do want to skim off your own cream, simply leave a large vat of milk in a wide pan at room temperature for 12–24 hours. Then use a utensil with lots of holes in it to skim the surface and collect all the floating cream. Cows' and ewes' milk will produce more cream than goats' milk.

Commercially, most cream is separated from milk by centrifugal force. This method was developed in the 19th century and involves spinning the milk around so that the heavy fat particles fly outwards first. There are various different types of cream available, depending on their fat content. Single cream contains 18 per cent fat, whipping cream has 35 per cent fat, double cream 48 per cent fat and clotted cream 55 per cent.

COOKING WITH MILK & CREAM

Both milk and cream complement a huge range of other flavours, in both sweet and savoury dishes. We avoid heating them for lengthy periods of time unless we are making custard. They are usually added to a dish in the final stages of cooking, at a low heat.

The key thing to remember is that milk and cream are always ready to change form. In many ways they are the chameleons of the kitchen and a little too much heat, acid or beating will transform not only the colour but also the taste and texture. For this reason, be scientific when working with dairy and try to pay attention to the little details that can result in success or failure.

SOURING MILK & CREAM

When bacterial cultures or rennet are added to milk or cream, they become sour and curdle because the bacteria help to convert the lactose sugars into lactic acid. This is the cornerstone of making cheese and yoghurt, as we shall find out later in the book. Lemon juice can also be used for souring and has the same effect. Cream or milk that has been cultured develops an acidic tang that is synonymous with yoghurt and cheese.

STORING MILK & CREAM

Store fresh milk and cream below 4°C (39°F) in sealed and sterilized containers. If you are intending to keep it any longer than 2 or 3 weeks, milk and cream should be frozen. Remove the air if using plastic freezer bags, seal tightly and place in the fast freezing section. Use within 2 months.

Everyone has a favourite milkshake flavour. Ours is a classic strawberry shake with banana for added depth and a hint of vanilla to add the extra wow factor. The milk should be ice cold; if it's not, add a handful of crushed ice to reduce the temperature.

SERVES 2

12-14 ripe strawberries, halved

1 tablespoon caster sugar

600ml (1 pint) whole or semi-skimmed milk

1 banana, roughly chopped

½ teaspoon vanilla extract or a pinch of vanilla seeds

2 scoops of vanilla ice cream (optional)

crushed ice

sprigs of fresh mint, to decorate

STRAWBERRY MILKSHAKE

Place the strawberries in a shallow bowl and sprinkle with the sugar. Set aside for 10 minutes.

Place all of the ingredients in a food processor and blend until smooth and creamy. Transfer to 2 large glasses, sprinkle with crushed ice, top each with a sprig of mint and serve with a straw.

The infused milk in this vibrant soup is herby, rich and aromatic and complements the metallic spinach. If anything, this is a milk soup first and a spinach soup second.

SERVES 4-6

50g (2oz) butter

1 onion, diced

2 garlic cloves, finely chopped

1 parsnip, peeled and diced

50ml (2fl oz) white wine

500g (1lb) spinach, rinsed and drained

goats' cheese, crumbled, to serve

FOR THE INFUSED MILK

6-8 cloves

½ onion, peeled

750ml (1¼ pints) whole goats' milk

3 black peppercorns

1 bay leaf

1 sprig each of parsley, thyme and sage

a pinch of grated nutmeg

salt and freshly ground black pepper

FOR THE CROUTONS

4 slices of stale bread, cut into cubes

2 tablespoons extra virgin olive oil

a pinch of rock salt or sea salt

FOR THE PARSNIP CRISPS

1 parsnip, peeled and finely sliced

vegetable oil, for deep-frying

SPINACH SOUP

To infuse the milk, insert the cloves into the onion and place all the ingredients in a pan. Heat slowly over a medium heat until hot but not boiling. Turn off the heat and leave to infuse for 20–30 minutes. Season to taste and strain through a fine sieve.

Melt the butter in a large pan over a medium heat and cook the onion and garlic until softened. Meanwhile, cook the parsnip in a pan of lightly salted boiling water until almost cooked. Drain and add to the pan with the onion, then add the wine. Reduce the heat and simmer gently for 10 minutes. Add the spinach and cook until wilted, then remove from the heat. Transfer the vegetables to a food processor and blend with the infused milk until smooth. Return to the pan and heat gently until hot but not boiling.

Meanwhile, make the croutons. Toss the bread cubes in a bowl with the olive oil, then sprinkle with salt. Fry in a hot pan until golden brown, then set aside to drain on kitchen paper.

To make the parsnip crisps, heat some vegetable oil to 190°C (375°F) in a deep-fryer or a large pan. Deep-fry the slices for about 45 seconds, or until crisp, then set aside to drain on kitchen paper.

Serve in warmed soup bowls, sprinkled with crumbled goats' cheese and croutons and topped with parsnip crisps.

Panna cotta is a cooked cream dessert which is guaranteed to impress. Our version adds perfumed lavender to the cream and makes the dish sweetly fragrant. The blueberry compote creates an extra fruity layer to enhance the delicate cream.

SERVES 6-8

FOR THE PANNA COTTA

1 tablespoon water

6g (¼oz) powdered gelatine

450ml (¾pint) single cream

1 sprig of lavender, plus extra to decorate (optional)

35g (1½oz) caster sugar

shortbread, to serve

FOR THE BLUEBERRY COMPOTE

175g (6oz) blueberries

100ml (3½fl oz) sparkling wine

25g (1oz) caster sugar

LAVENDER PANNA COTTA

Pour the water into a small cup and sprinkle the gelatine evenly over it. Set aside to soak.

Heat the cream and lavender in a pan over a medium heat until hot but not boiling, then remove from the heat and leave to infuse for 20–30 minutes. Add the sugar and return to the heat. Stir until the sugar has dissolved but do not allow it to boil. Remove from the heat and allow to cool for 2–3 minutes, then remove the lavender sprig and stir in the soaked gelatine. Stir until smooth, then divide between 6–8 small glasses, leaving a 1–2cm (½–1 inch) gap at the top of each. Allow to cool, then chill in the refrigerator for 2 hours until set.

To make the blueberry compote, place all the ingredients in a pan, bring to the boil, then reduce the heat and simmer gently for 30 minutes. Blend in a food processor until smooth, then pass through a sieve and allow to cool. Pour the compote over the set panna cotta, decorate with extra lavender flowers, if liked, and serve with shortbread.

When we visit our family in Northern Ireland, we drink this coffee in the evening while catching up around the peat fire. The whiskey provides warmth and depth to the sweetened coffee and the whipped cream floats sublimely on top, providing a cool contrast to the heated debate going on below. The key to making hot whiskey drinks is not to waste a good Irish malt, but use blended whiskey instead.

SERVES 1

1 measure of Irish whiskey

2 teaspoons brown sugar

1 cup of fresh black coffee

50ml (2fl oz) double cream, softly whipped

IRISH COFFEE

Place the whiskey and sugar in a short glass and stir together with a metal spoon. The sugar is essential to help the cream float on top of the coffee, so don't leave it out. Leave the spoon in as you pour in the hot coffee as it will prevent the glass from cracking due to the sudden change in temperature. Stir well, then spoon the whipped cream on top. Serve immediately.

soft peaks make the perfect whipped cream

SOURED CREAM

Making soured cream is a great way to understand the basics of using bacterial cultures. The process is quick, simple and easily achievable at home. Soured cream has a lovely mild, sour flavour due to the lactic acid produced by the bacterial culture added to the cream to sour it. Sachets of freeze-dried soured cream and crème fraîche starter cultures are readily available online and offer an easy route to creating these lovely products.

PREPARING

You will need a number of glass jars with lids, which should be sterilized (see page 14) before use. You will also need a water bath (see page 12) in which to warm and ripen the cream (see page 72). You can use either a mesophilic starter culture or a special soured cream starter.

MAKING

The cream is poured into the sterilized jars and heated in the water bath to the correct temperature. The culture is then added (see page 14) and left in the warm cream to sour it. The soured cream then has to be left at warm room temperature for a further 24 hours for the culture to develop, so it is best to make soured cream in winter when you have the heating on, or in summer on a warm day. The soured cream is ready when it thickens to the consistency of pouring yoghurt.

STORING

Soured cream improves when left for 2–3 days in the refrigerator. The unopened jars will keep for up to 3 weeks. Once opened, though, consume within 3–5 days. Store soured cream in multiple pots so that you only need to open what you will use.

NOW TRY: BUTTERMILK SOURED CREAM

This is a quick and easy way to make soured cream. Mix 350ml (12fl oz) of double cream, 350ml (12fl oz) of whole cows' milk and 175ml (6fl oz) of cultured buttermilk, pour into sterilized jars and place in a water bath. Follow the instructions for making and storing standard soured cream, but heat the water to just 24°C (75°F) before turning off the heat.

NOW TRY: CRÈME FRAÎCHE

Crème fraîche is less tangy than soured cream and doesn't curdle when it is heated. An easy way to make your own crème fraîche at home is to buy a small pot and use it as a starter culture to sour some double cream. This works with the majority of crème fraîche, but avoid crème fraîche made with raw milk, which is pasteurized after it is cultured. Stir 1 tablespoon of crème fraîche into 350ml (12fl oz) of double cream, cover and leave at warm room temperature, 25–30°C (77–86°F), for 24 hours. Store in the refrigerator for up to 3 weeks.

You can also make soured cream in the same way, by adding some commercial soured cream to fresh double cream.

HOW TO MAKE SOURED CREAM

Pour the cream into glass jars and place in a water bath. Heat slowly over a period of 15–20 minutes until it reaches 30°C (86°F).

Turn off the heat and sprinkle the starter over the surface. Leave for 5 minutes, then stir in gently using a whisk.

SIMPLE SOURED CREAM

Makes 1 litre (1¾ pints)

1 litre (1¾ pints) single cream

⅛ teaspoon mesophilic or soured cream starter culture

To make soured cream, follow the instructions above and opposite.

Place the lids loosely on the jars and leave in the water bath for 12 hours. Then seal the lids and leave in the water bath at warm room temperature for a further 24 hours.

Soured cream is excellent drizzled on a whole range of exciting dishes. We use it on nachos, tacos and all sorts of Tex-Mex food, but we especially love to use it with popcorn. Popcorn is extremely easy to make at home and this combination of soured cream and chives is our favourite flavour.

SERVES 6

2 tablespoons groundnut oil

100g (3½oz) popping corn

2 tablespoons butter

2 tablespoons soured cream

1 teaspoon crushed garlic

2 tablespoons finely chopped fresh chives

salt

SOURED CREAM & CHIVE POPCORN

Heat the oil in a large pan with a lid, then add the corn, cover and shake over a high heat for 3 minutes, or according to the packet instructions, until the popping has stopped.

Melt the butter in a small pan, add the soured cream, garlic and most of the chives. Pour the mixture over the warm popcorn and toss to coat evenly.

Arrange the popcorn on a lightly greased baking tray and cook under a preheated medium grill for 1–2 minutes, taking care not to burn it. Transfer to a large bowl and sprinkle with a pinch of salt and the remaining chives.

Clotted cream is deliciously rich and irresistibly golden. Many farms in the south-west of England specialize in making this traditional thick cream to serve with scones or make into ice cream. We have always assumed that the process was complicated but recent visits to dairies have led us to discover that you can achieve your own delicious clotted cream at home with no special ingredients or equipment. The secret is in the gentle clotting or cooking of the cream.

MAKES 100-200G (3½-7OZ)

1 litre (1¾ pints) double cream

CLOTTED CREAM

Preheat the oven to 90°C (200°F), just below Gas Mark ¼. Pour the cream into a shallow ovenproof dish and cook in the oven for 2 hours. Allow to cool, then chill in the refrigerator for 24 hours, by which time a golden crust will have formed on the surface.

Slice the clotted cream into segments and use a fish slice to transfer it to a container with a lid. The liquid cream left behind can be used in cooking. Serve the clotted cream on freshly baked scones with jam or marmalade, and consume within 1–2 weeks.

It should fold as you peel a layer off

use pretty tea cups to delight your guests

METHOD #2

TRADITIONAL SET CUSTARD

The thick creamy taste and smooth golden texture of custard is very special, and the old-fashioned way of making set custards in the oven is worth celebrating. The skills involved in making custard are useful to attain as the same principles can be applied to making sweet pastries, ice creams, desserts and even savoury dishes.

PREPARING

The key elements in custard are eggs and milk or cream. The method simply involves heating these ingredients so that the eggs set the liquid. Never overheat your custard or it will turn into scrambled eggs suspended in whey.

MAKING

Start by heating the milk or cream in a heavy-based pan. Warm it slowly over a low heat and turn it off before it comes to the boil. Then pour the hot liquid very slowly over the eggs, which have been whisked in a mixing bowl. It is important to keep whisking while you add the hot liquid to keep the temperature consistent. Gradually the mixture will become silky smooth. If you are worried the liquid is too hot, pour it slowly down the side of the mixing bowl as you add it to reduce the temperature as it goes, whisking all the while.

USING A BAIN-MARIE

At this stage, the custard mixture could be returned to the pan and heated very slowly over a low heat to create runny custard. However, using a bain-marie to make traditional set custards takes some of the risk away as the heat applied is a lot more gentle.

Pour the custard into individual ramekins or cups and place on a wire rack or folded tea towel in a shallow roasting tin. Fill the tin with hot water to half or two-thirds of the way up the sides of the cups. The rack or folded tea towel will prevent direct heat from the bottom of the pan burning the custards and the water ensures a consistent temperature around them.

THE SET TEST

To check whether the custards are ready, tilt one of the cups at a 45° angle: the custard should stay put. Alternatively, dip a knife near the centre of the custard: it should come out fairly clean.

STORING

Cover the surfaces of the custards with clingfilm or greaseproof paper as they cool to prevent a skin forming. Leave to cool at room temperature for 30–40 minutes, then refrigerate for up to 2–3 days until ready to serve.

HOW TO MAKE SET CUSTARD CUPS

Whisk the egg yolks and sugar in a large bowl until well combined. Heat the cream or milk in a pan over a medium heat until just starting to simmer.

Slowly pour the cream or milk on to the egg mixture, whisking all the time until the sugar has dissolved. Split the vanilla pod, remove the seeds and add them to the custard.

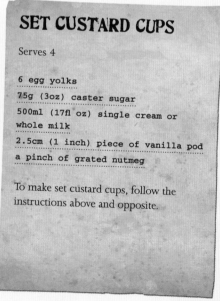

SET CUSTARD CUPS

Serves 4

6 egg yolks

75g (3oz) caster sugar

500ml (17fl oz) single cream or whole milk

2.5cm (1 inch) piece of vanilla pod

a pinch of grated nutmeg

To make set custard cups, follow the instructions above and opposite.

Pour into 4 ovenproof cups, dust with nutmeg and cover with foil. Cook in a bain-marie in a preheated oven at 160°C (325°F), Gas Mark 3, for 45–60 minutes until set.

The crisp puff pastry enclosing these tarts is delicious with the creamy, lemon-and cinnamon-scented custard inside. The fact that they are only small seems to cancel out any guilt associated with eating them. The only problem is that one is never enough!

MAKES 12

250g (8oz) caster sugar

2 slices of lemon

2 cinnamon sticks

100ml (3½fl oz) water

25g (1oz) plain flour, plus extra for dusting

25g (1oz) cornflour

2-3 drops of vanilla extract

250ml (8fl oz) semi-skimmed milk

1 egg, plus 3 egg yolks, beaten

butter, for greasing

icing sugar, for dusting

350g (11½oz) puff pastry

PORTUGUESE CUSTARD TARTS

Place the sugar, lemon and cinnamon in a pan with the water and heat gently, stirring, until the sugar dissolves. Bring to the boil and remove from the heat.

Place the flour, cornflour and vanilla in a mixing bowl, add a little of the milk and mix to a smooth paste. Place the remaining milk in another pan and bring just to the boil. Pour over the flour mixture, whisking well to combine, then return to the pan and cook gently over a medium heat, whisking continuously, until the mixture thickens and starts to simmer.

Remove the lemon slices and cinnamon sticks from the syrup and pour into the milk mixture. Stir together, then add the eggs. Bring slowly back to a simmer, whisking until smooth and thickened. Pour into a jug, cover the surface of the custard with clingfilm or greaseproof paper and allow to cool.

Preheat the oven to 220°C (425°F), Gas Mark 7, and grease a 12-hole muffin tray. Place a baking sheet in the oven to heat up. Lightly dust a work surface with flour and icing sugar and roll out the puff pastry into a large rectangle, about 12–24cm (5–9 inches) wide. Fold the pastry in half, then roll up like a Swiss roll. Cut the roll into 12 slices 1–2cm (½– ¾ inch) thick.

Lay each of the pastry slices flat on the work surface and roll out to a 10cm (4 inch) round. Press a round of pastry into each of the holes in the muffin tray and divide the cooled custard between them. Place the muffin tray on the baking sheet in the oven and cook for 20 minutes until puffed and golden. Allow to cool in the tin. Dust with icing sugar.

2

BUTTER

INTRODUCTION TO

BUTTER

Traditionally, people would make butter as part of their domestic routine. Using all the milk and cream from the family cow was a full-time job and it couldn't afford to be wasted! Nowadays you don't need your own cow or even a well-equipped dairy to create delicious salted or unsalted butter at home. Butter can be made from more than just cows' milk. Butters made with goats' or ewes' milk are much paler in colour but the taste is remarkably similar.

TOOLS & EQUIPMENT

A glass jar with a screw-on lid is all you really need for a basic butter churn as simply shaking the cream will eventually separate the butter fat from the buttermilk. However, there are other churning options that are a little easier on the muscles, and some other pieces of equipment you might like to buy.

CHURNS

Traditionally, churning was done using a special drum-shaped churn with a big turning handle, or another device a bit like a giant plunger. These can still be found in second-hand shops, but they would need to be cleaned thoroughly before use. There are also modern equivalents available from specialist shops online, and the hand-powered varieties have a retro charm. However, an egg whisk or food processor will do the job, too. If the cream is at the right temperature (about 20°C/68°F) then the butter will 'come' (the term for when it changes from cream to butter) in a matter of minutes.

BUTTER PATS

Butter pats are small wooden bats used to squeeze the whey out of the butter. The grooves in the surface allow the liquid to run away. Again, these great old-fashioned utensils can be bought in second-hand shops, and there are modern equivalents, but a spatula and wooden chopping board could also be used for the job.

MOULDS & STAMPS

Butter moulds are also available from dairy suppliers and second-hand shops and are used to shape the butter into attractive shapes once it is made. A simple plastic tub will do, or the butter can simply be formed into a pat instead. We have also bought a few original stamps to decorate the top of the butter before it is chilled.

SALTED OR UNSALTED?

Salted butter will keep for a few days longer than unsalted butter. We tend to add salt to improve the taste but also to prevent the butter from turning rancid too quickly.

SHAPING BUTTER

Butter can be shaped in attractive moulds, rolled in paper into cylinders, spread into ramekins or left in a rectangular pat. All these options are easy to do; you just need to work your freshly churned butter into shape and set in the refrigerator to firm up.

Frozen rolls of butter are easier to carve into rounds

MAKING BUTTER SAUCES

Using your own butter in a rich and delicious sauce is the ultimate home-cooking experience. A butter sauce can be almost entirely made from butter, flavoured by adding a few extra ingredients, or by cooking it to change the flavour.

Heating butter in a small pan and adding lemon juice will give you a sharp sauce called a beurre meunière; adding white wine, chopped shallots and some cream will create the famous beurre blanc; and a beurre noisette is simply butter that tastes nutty after cooking (see page 52).

We treat butter as a sauce in itself, using a knob of flavoured butter to dress meat, fish and vegetables with added depth.

METHOD #3

BUTTER

Butter is a key ingredient in so many dishes but people rarely make their own at home. In fact, it is extremely quick and easy to make a basic butter without any specialist equipment. The whole process takes a few minutes and you end up with a pat of your own butter, seasoned exactly to your taste. You can even get creative and combine your favourite flavourings into the freshly churned mixture. We use a food processor for churning, which may sound a bit like cheating, but it guarantees good results every time.

PREPARING

Whatever you choose to use for churning the butter (see page 42), be sure to sterilize it (see page 14) before you begin. It also helps to start with the cream at around 20°C (68°F), so remove it from the refrigerator to warm up before you make your butter.

MAKING

To make butter, soured cream is churned or whisked until the fat comes together into clusters, separating itself from the surrounding buttermilk. This process is so basic that it is difficult to believe it could be so simple. Once you have poured off the liquid, it is time to wash and squeeze the butter to remove all traces of cream and buttermilk from it. This process is vital to prevent the butter from turning rancid later.

We use butter pats for the job, using them rather like a trowel that you mix mortar with when building. This may sound a bit industrial and not suited to the sterile environment of a home dairy but the approach needs to be firm. Work deftly and you will eventually get very used to the skill.

STORING

Keep the butter in the refrigerator and consume within 3 weeks. If your butter turns rancid soon after making, it is probably the result of pockets of liquid remaining among the butter fats. Next time you make a batch, squeeze out as much of the washing water and buttermilk as you can. Butter can be frozen for up to 3 months and used straight from the freezer. Try rolling it into a log and slicing it before freezing so you can remove a round or two to melt on to some hot grilled fish or a steak as you need it.

NOW TRY: BUTTERMILK

Buttermilk is the liquid left behind after churning butter from cream. It has a creamy texture and a delicious tangy taste. Once you've churned the butter, strain the buttermilk through a fine sieve (see page 47) and store it in the refrigerator for up to a week.

NOW TRY: CLARIFIED BUTTER

If you want your butter to last even longer in the refrigerator, you can clarify it to remove more of the moisture from the fat. A layer of clarified butter is traditionally used to cover pâtés and potted shrimps to keep out the air and preserve them for longer. Cut the butter into small cubes and place in a heavy-based pan over a low heat. Cook for 10–15 minutes without stirring until the fat and water separate. Pour off the yellow fat through a fine sieve into a bowl and keep in the refrigerator for up to 6 weeks.

NOW TRY: GHEE

Ghee is an Indian clarified butter with a nuttier taste. Follow the instructions above but cook for longer until the solids separate out and the flavour intensifies. Ghee can be kept in the refrigerator for 3–4 months and will transform your homemade curries.

NOW TRY: ADDING FLAVOURINGS

Butter can be transformed into an instant sauce or garnish by blending with herbs, spices and other ingredients. Flatten the butter into a rectangle on a sheet of greaseproof paper, sprinkle the flavourings over the top and roll up the butter to form a cylinder. Wrap up and store in the freezer until you need a slice. Use to sauté with onions, melt over grilled fish or meat, or add to mashed potatoes.

Salt, pepper and thyme Mix 1 teaspoon each of sea salt, fresh thyme and pink peppercorns with 100g (3½oz) of butter.

Mixed herbes de Provence Combine 1–2 teaspoons of mixed chopped fresh fennel, basil, thyme and savory with 100g (3½oz) of butter – perfect for braising meat or serving with warm bread and vegetable stews.

Garlic and parsley Add 1–2 crushed garlic cloves and 1 teaspoon of chopped fresh parsley to 100g (3½oz) of butter for a great shortcut to garlic bread. Simply slice a baguette in several places and insert a round of flavoured butter in each cut.

Horseradish Mix 1 teaspoon of grated horseradish with 100g (3½oz) of butter. A cold disc melting on a flame-grilled steak is very hard to beat.

SALTED BUTTER

Makes 1 litre (1¾ pints)

1.2 litres (2 pints) extra
thick double cream
3 teaspoons live natural yogurt
sea salt

To make butter, follow the
instructions opposite and on pages
44–45. For unsalted butter, skip
step 6.

HOW TO MAKE BUTTER

Pour the thick double cream into a sterilized
bowl or a food processor and add the live
natural yogurt.

Pour cold water over the butter, then squeeze
it using butter pats or a spatula and board
to remove all traces of liquid. Wash again
and repeat.

Continue washing and squeezing the butter
until all traces of cream and buttermilk have
gone and the liquid runs clear, not cloudy.

Use a whisk or switch on the food processor to work the mixture until it forms soft peaks. Continue whisking or blending until it resembles scrambled eggs.

Soon after the butter will 'come' and turn into small globules of fat surrounded by buttermilk. Pour off the buttermilk and reserve for use in another recipe.

Weigh the butter, then weigh out 2 per cent of its weight in salt. Spread the butter out flat, sprinkle the salt over the top and work it into the butter with a spatula.

Shape the butter into a pat and place in a plastic container. Alternatively, roll it up in a twist of paper or ram it down hard into a butter mould to expel any air.

Truffles are an indulgent treat we often make for parties and gatherings to serve with our coffee. However, truffles don't always have to be sweet: this cheesy version is perfect with drinks to kick off proceedings, or makes a bold statement on the cheese board.

SERVES 12

250g (8oz) unsalted butter, softened

200g (7oz) goats' cheese or Gouda

½ teaspoon salt

a pinch of grated nutmeg

a pinch of cayenne pepper

a dash of Worcestershire sauce

FOR THE COATINGS

toasted pumpernickel breadcrumbs

crushed pine nuts or pecans

smoked paprika

finely chopped fresh chives

CHEESE TRUFFLES

Place all the truffle ingredients in a food processor and blend until smooth. Use a small scoop or a spoon to form a ball, then roll the mixture into 2.5cm (1 inch) balls. Sprinkle the coatings on separate plates and roll the truffles in them until evenly coated. Chill in the refrigerator for at least 1 hour, then serve in petit four cases.

Consume any leftover truffles within 1–2 weeks. Truffles with fresh herb coatings won't last as long as those rolled in spices or dried herbs, so eat the herb-covered truffles within 4–5 days.

Roll gently to coat your truffles

Breakfast isn't complete without one of Granny's buttermilk pancakes, topped with butter and a drizzle of maple syrup. This is a great way to use up the buttermilk after you've made butter. For many years we've enjoyed these traditional pancakes and now we can share the top-secret family recipe.

SERVES 4–6

250g (8oz) plain flour

½ teaspoon bicarbonate of soda

½ teaspoon cream of tartar

¼ teaspoon salt

1 large egg

75g (3oz) caster sugar

500ml (17fl oz) buttermilk

butter, for greasing

GRANNY'S BUTTERMILK PANCAKES

Place the flour in a bowl with the bicarbonate of soda, cream of tartar and salt. Mix thoroughly and set aside.

Beat the egg in a mixing bowl and add the sugar. Beat well with a wooden spoon to combine, then sift in the flour a little at a time and stir well. Gradually pour in the buttermilk and beat to form a smooth batter. Set aside with a ladle at the ready.

Heat a griddle pan until moderately hot, then wipe the surface with a smear of butter on a piece of kitchen paper. Pour a ladleful of batter on to the griddle and cook for 1–2 minutes until bubbles rise to the surface. Turn over and cook the other side for 30 seconds until golden. If the pancake cooks too quickly or too slowly, adjust the temperature before you cook the remaining pancakes. Wrap the cooked pancakes in a clean tea towel until you are ready to serve.

This is probably our favourite butter sauce due to its sheer simplicity, golden appearance and unmistakable nutty aroma. If you add some lemon juice to the sauce, it becomes beurre meunière, but we prefer to drizzle our lemon juice over the cooked fish sitting in its glistening pool of nut-brown butter. This sauce can also be served with chargrilled asparagus, poached chicken, rose veal or medallions of pork fillet.

SERVES 2

100g (3½oz) butter

salt and freshly ground black pepper

4 lemon sole fillets

FOR THE TOPPING

1 teaspoon olive oil

2 tablespoons wafer-thin slices of broccoli

50g (2oz) pine nuts, roughly crushed

zest and juice of 1 lemon

1 tablespoon chopped fresh parsley

2 tablespoons capers

TO SERVE

a handful of watercress

buttered new potatoes

LEMON SOLE WITH BEURRE NOISETTE

Heat the butter in a nonstick frying pan over a medium heat and cook until it turns golden and the distinctive nutty smell rises from the pan. Add a pinch of salt and pepper, then remove from the heat and pour the sauce into a jug.

Return the pan to the stove and turn up the heat to high. Season the fish fillets and add to the pan, skin side down. Sear for 1–2 minutes, then reduce the heat and turn the fish over. Drizzle the beurre noisette over the fish and cook for a further 2–3 minutes until the fish is just cooked through.

Meanwhile, for the topping, heat the oil in a frying pan over a high heat and add the broccoli, pine nuts, capers, parsley and lemon zest. Cook for 2 minutes, then add the lemon juice and season to taste.

Divide the watercress between 2 serving plates and arrange the fish on top. Pour over the beurre noisette and sprinkle with the broccoli topping. Serve immediately with buttered new potatoes.

3

YOGHURT

INTRODUCTION TO

YOGHURT

Yoghurt is milk that has been transformed into a soft curd by the action of lactic acid bacteria. Think of the bacteria as back-up singers that support the milk, transforming it from a solo singer into a harmonious group. Yoghurt can be strained for a firmer consistency or flavoured with fruit to add colour and taste, but the best part is that homemade yoghurt is really good for you. In fact, some of the words for yoghurt around the world implicate long life and good health. All we know is that you get a good feeling in your gut when you eat homemade yoghurt -- and the taste ain't bad either!

FROM MILK TO YOGHURT

Making yoghurt is simply a case of adding the right friendly bacteria to some milk and keeping the milk at the right temperature for them to thrive. The micro-organisms convert the milk sugars into lactic acid, which curdles the milk proteins and gives yoghurt its distinctive texture and tangy flavour.

Making your own at home is relatively simple as long as you use sterilized equipment to prevent other bacteria thriving. Another useful tip is to heat your milk first and then cool it down before adding in the starter culture. This ripens the milk ready for the bacteria to thrive and also kills off any unwanted bacteria that may be around.

FRIENDLY BACTERIA

The bacteria can be added in the form of a spoonful of live yoghurt, or a special powdered yoghurt starter culture, available online from dairy suppliers. Live natural yoghurt is obviously easier to buy, but commercial freeze-dried starters are more reliable and reduce the chance of just ending up with a batch of soured milk.

The bacteria in live yoghurt normally include one or all of *Lactobacillus bulgaricus*, *Lactobacillus acidopholis* and *Streptococcus thermophilis*. These all have a positive effect on internal health, in particular the digestive system. They are all tolerant of the kitchen environment and will grow at temperatures between 36°C (97°F) and 55°C (131°F). The ideal temperature range is 40–50°C (104–122°F), and this is what we try to achieve when making yoghurt.

ADDING FLAVOURINGS

Perhaps the most exciting part of making your own yoghurt is adding flavours to it so that you can compete with the huge range of different yoghurts available in shops. Add your chosen flavouring ingredients after the yoghurt has been made. Stir them in gently, trying to avoid breaking the delicate curds, and return to the refrigerator to firm up again afterwards. If there is some separation of curds and whey as you stir, pour away some of the unwanted liquid. Another option is to place your flavouring ingredients in the bottom of the pots and pour your freshly made yoghurt on top before storing in the refrigerator.

A guilt-free way to start the day

METHOD #4

YOGHURT

We see homemade yoghurt as a great way to learn about bacteria and starter cultures before moving on to more complex methods in cheese-making. Yoghurt can be made using any milk -- goats' milk will create a softer consistency and different flavour to cows' milk. The benefit of making your own is that it is far cheaper than buying yoghurt, even when you use organic milk.

PREPARING

Start by buying a tub of live natural yoghurt, or ordering some sachets of yoghurt starter culture online. The freeze-dried cultures are likely to include at least two of the three main yoghurt bacteria: *Lactobacillus bulgaricus*, *Lactobacillus acidophilus* and *Streptococcus thermophilus*. These give live yoghurt its distinctive taste and texture.

Goats' milk makes much runnier yoghurt than cows' milk, more of a pouring yoghurt, so you can add a drop of rennet to goats' milk yoghurt if you want a firmer texture.

Before you start you also need to sterilize your equipment (see page 14).

MAKING

Making yoghurt is all about maintaining the right temperature for the bacteria to thrive for a number of hours (see page 72), so they can sour the milk and develop that delicious taste and texture. One simple solution is an old-fashioned vacuum flask. This can be placed in a warm part of the kitchen and is ideal for making small batches of yoghurt. If you don't have a vacuum flask, wrap the container with the yoghurt in a thick towel and leave somewhere warm.

There is another more high-tech option in the form of a commercial yoghurt maker. These simple machines are convenient and affordable and they are excellent at maintaining the correct temperature while the bacteria work their magic. Some yoghurt makers are like vacuum flasks and require the milk to be heated first, other electric machines do this for you.

STORING

Store yoghurt in the refrigerator at less than 4°C (39°F) and consume within 10 days. Alternatively, make into frozen yoghurt (see page 66).

BASIC YOGHURT

Makes 1 litre (1¾ pints)

1 litre (1¾ pints) whole cows' milk

1 sachet of yoghurt starter culture or 75ml (3fl oz) live natural yoghurt

1 drop of rennet, mixed with 1 teaspoon sterilized water (for goats' milk only)

To make yoghurt, follow the instructions above and opposite.

HOW TO MAKE YOGHURT

Heat the milk slowly in a water bath over a period of 30 minutes until it reaches 40–50°C (104–122°F).

Turn off the heat, sprinkle the starter over the surface and leave for 5 minutes. Alternatively, simply add the live yoghurt. Add the rennet, if using.

Whisk the milk in up and down motions to combine, then transfer to sterilized containers or a vacuum flask and seal. Keep at 40–50°C (104–122°F) for 6 hours.

If using a vacuum flask, transfer the yoghurt to a sterilized container with a lid. Place the yoghurt in the refrigerator to set further.

Kefir is a refreshing fermented drink that is traditionally made using kefir grains, which are added to fresh milk and left in a bag to ferment. These days, kefir can be made using a bacterial starter culture. It has superb health benefits due to the particular strains of beneficial bacteria it contains.

MAKES 1 LITRE (1¾ PINTS)

1 litre (1¾ pints) whole cows' milk

½ teaspoon or 1 sachet of kefir starter culture

KEFIR

Heat the milk slowly in a water bath over a low heat until it reaches 32°C (90°F). Turn off the heat, sprinkle the starter over the surface of the milk and leave for 5 minutes. Whisk the milk in up and down motions to combine, then transfer to sterilized containers and seal. Leave at room temperature for 12–24 hours while the milk ripens and the tangy flavour develops. The longer you leave it, the more pronounced the flavour, so if you haven't had kefir before start with just a short time. Store in the refrigerator and consume within 10 days.

To make more kefir, simply pour 50ml (2fl oz) of the fermented kefir into another 1 litre (1¾ pints) of warm milk and leave for a further 12 hours. This re-culturing can be repeated for up to 5 generations. After this you will need more dried starter culture.

Drink kefir a little at a time if you are new to the drink, then build up over a week or two. If you drink too much too quickly you may find your digestive system reacts unfavorably, so it's worth introducing it to your diet gradually.

Smooth, creamy and seductive →

METHOD #5

GREEK-STYLE YOGHURT

Greek yoghurt has a richer flavour and heavier texture than plain yogurt. This is brought about partly by the addition of cream and partly by draining off some of the whey to thicken it.

PREPARING

Greek yoghurt is made by adding some live yoghurt to a mixture of cream and milk, which has been heated to provide the perfect temperature for the bacteria in the yoghurt to grow. After the yoghurt has thickened, some of the whey is drained off to make it even thicker. This is done by placing the yoghurt milk solids in a colander lined with cheesecloth. To prepare a colander, line it with a double thickness of cheesecloth. The double thickness produces a finer mesh, particularly important with yoghurt as the milk solids are relatively small.

If you want to collect the whey to use it later for brining or cooking more complex cheeses, place a large bowl or pan under the colander. Whey tends to go sour very quickly, so use it or refrigerate it straight away.

DRAINING

This is a skill that will be repeated many times in this book with many types of cheese. The steps needed for a strained yoghurt like this are simple and don't take very long. Start by ladling out some of the whey from the surface of the yoghurt milk solids, then use a large ladle to lift out the exposed milk solids and transfer them to the lined colander. Once you

have ladled the milk solids into the colander, leave to drain for 20–30 minutes. The yoghurt is ready when there is little or no whey dripping from the base.

STORING & USING

Keep Greek yoghurt in a sealed container in the refrigerator and consume within a week. Serve plain in pitta breads with grilled lamb or chicken, or stir in a selection of herbs or spices, such as ras el hanout, to make a refreshing dip to accompany spicy North African dishes.

GREEK-STYLE YOGHURT

Makes about 500g (1lb)

500ml (17fl oz) whole cows' milk

500ml (17fl oz) double cream

1 drop of rennet, mixed with 1 teaspoon sterilized water

75ml (3fl oz) live natural yoghurt

To make Greek-style yoghurt, follow the instructions above and opposite.

HOW TO MAKE GREEK-STYLE YOGHURT

Heat the milk and cream slowly in a water bath over a period of 1 hour until it reaches 82°C (180°F), then transfer the pan to a bowl of iced water.

Whisk until the temperature drops to 38–40°C (100–104°F), then add the rennet and yoghurt. Stir well, then cover and leave for 6–8 hours at room temperature.

Stir with a rubber spatula for a few seconds to break the milk solids into large chunks, then cover again and leave for a further 10–15 minutes.

Transfer the milk solids to a cheesecloth-lined colander and leave for 20 minutes or until the whey stops dripping. Transfer to a container with a lid and chill to set further.

GOURMET YOGHURT POTS

EACH SERVES 4

For everyday yoghurt pots, we usually just add a swirl of honey with some nuts or fresh fruit. Here we have transformed our cool and creamy yoghurt into an enticing gourmet treat by adding some more unusual treats.

ROSE DELIGHT

50g (2oz) Turkish Delight

1 teaspoon fresh rose petals, roughly torn, plus extra to decorate

2 tablespoons flaked almonds, toasted

200ml (7fl oz) Greek-style yoghurt

Chop the Turkish Delight into small cubes. Divide the Turkish Delight, rose petals and almonds between the bases of 4 pots. Pour the yoghurt over the top and chill in the refrigerator for 2 hours. Serve decorated with a few extra rose petals.

PEANUT & APRICOT

50g (2oz) soft dried apricots

1 tablespoon honey

1 tablespoon peanut butter

200ml (7fl oz) Greek-style yoghurt

40g (1½oz) peanut brittle, chopped

Place the apricots and honey in a food processor and blend to a smooth paste. Mix with the peanut butter and swirl through the yoghurt. Divide between 4 pots and sprinkle the peanut brittle on top. Chill in the refrigerator for 2 hours.

RASPBERRY & LEMON VERBENA

6 sprigs of lemon verbena

100g (3½oz) raspberries

20g (¾oz) caster sugar

1 tablespoon water

200ml (7fl oz) Greek-style yoghurt

1 tablespoon crème de framboise

Place 2 sprigs of lemon verbena, the raspberries, sugar and water in a pan over a medium heat and cook for 15 minutes. Pass the mixture through a sieve and leave to cool. Stir gently into the yoghurt, then divide between 4 pots. Drizzle the crème de framboise over the top and stir very lightly to create a ripple effect. Chill in the refrigerator for 2 hours. Serve decorated with the remaining sprigs of lemon verbena.

Like good coffee, frozen yoghurt can be made at home with little effort – that's why we have decided to combine the two in this quick and easy recipe. Like ice cream and sorbet recipes, you can substitute a vast range of flavours using the same basic technique.

SERVES 5-6

500ml (17fl oz) Greek-style yoghurt

250ml (8fl oz) milk

50g (2oz) caster sugar

50ml (2fl oz) cold espresso coffee

65g (2½oz) biscotti, crushed

50g (2oz) chocolate-covered coffee beans, plus extra to serve

1 tablespoon cocoa powder, for dusting

FROZEN CAPPUCCINO YOGHURT

Whisk the yoghurt, milk and sugar with the coffee until evenly combined. Chill in the refrigerator for at least 2 hours before transferring to an ice cream machine for churning and freezing.

Alternatively, to make by hand, pour the mixture into a shallow freezerproof container and place in the freezer. Remove every 30–40 minutes for 2–3 hours and use a fork to beat the mixture and break up the ice crystals around the edges.

When the mixture is smooth and creamy, add the crushed biscotti and coffee beans and stir until evenly distributed. Freeze for at least 2 hours before serving in coffee cups with a dusting of cocoa powder and a couple of chocolate-covered coffee beans on the side.

CHEESE

INTRODUCTION TO
CHEESE

We love eating cheese and sampling the huge range of different types on offer. Most cultures around the world make cheese using traditional methods passed down through the generations. Artisan cheese-makers everywhere use the milk available to them and the local environmental conditions to create unique and distinctive flavours. Cheese has a rich history and the art of making it has developed over hundreds of years. Because of this heritage you may feel a slight sense of trepidation at the thought of making your own. We say you've got to start somewhere, so jump in with both feet and have a go!

MAKING A START

Making cheese is unlike other areas of cookery where an improvised attitude and confident approach can succeed. For cheese to form, last well and taste good, you need to follow a basic set of principles, which are outlined in this chapter. That's not to say that it isn't fun – there is plenty of room to experiment with flavours and textures later, while still following the basic rules of hygiene and respecting certain scientific principles.

Keeping control of the temperature, pH levels and living bacterial cultures all make cheese-making a meticulous art, so start at the beginning with simple soft cheese and learn the basic principles. Once you feel like an accomplished soft cheese-maker, move on to the next level and master more classic skills. We have visited many professional cheese-makers and spent time learning some of the tricks of the trade. All this knowledge can be broken down into a simple code of cheese-making: stay clean, be organized, follow the instructions carefully, plan ahead and smile lots.

CHEESE-MAKING EQUIPMENT

There are many cheese-making suppliers online, offering a huge selection of products, gadgets, moulds, presses and tools that are used by professionals. You may want to invest in some of this equipment if you intend to make cheese regularly, but we would recommend starting off with the basics and making cheese in small batches. For this you can improvise with ordinary kitchen utensils. When you progress to more complex methods and cheeses with distinctive shapes, you may want to invest in some of the following items:

- **Cheesecloth:** This fine gauzy fabric is used for draining the whey from the curds and for wrapping cheeses as they ripen. You can also buy cheese-draining sacks made from the same fabric, which are useful for hanging, but we tend to use squares of cheesecloth and draw up the corners to make our own.
- **Cheese iron:** This is a simple tool that is inserted into a hard cheese to take a sample to gauge whether the cheese is ready to eat.
- **Cheese mat:** This is a sheet of plastic mesh on which cheeses are placed for ripening

Variety is the spice of life - get different shapes and sizes

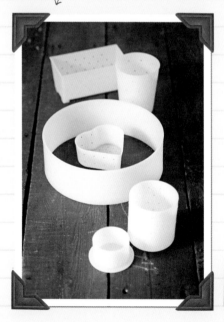

and ageing. It is designed to hold the cheese just off the surface below to allow moisture to drain away.

- **Cheese moulds:** These come in all shapes and sizes for making many different types of cheese. We own several moulds to suit the traditional shapes of the cheeses we are making, but most soft cheeses are extremely rustic and require very little of this sort of thing. We also make moulds by drilling a series of drainage holes in simple plastic containers.
- **Cheese press:** These simple contraptions are used to press the moisture out of hard cheeses. They are very effective, but other heavy items can be used instead, such as cans of food or bottles of water.
- **Cheese wax:** You will need special cheese wax if you want to cover your cheeses (see pages 150–1). Cheese wax is available in a number of different colours.
- **Curd cutter:** This tool comprises a number of equally spaced blades, used to cut the curd into regular pieces. A palette knife is a good substitute.
- **Heat-resistant gloves:** These will be needed when making cheese such as mozzarella.
- **PH testing equipment:** When making some types of cheese, for example mozzarella, you need to monitor the acidity level as this is crucial to success. This can be done using a digital pH meter, which is fast and accurate but more expensive, or pH testing strips which are cheaper and readily available from cheese-making suppliers. Make sure that when you buy these they are able to show a range of 4.9–5.2, the exact parameters for perfect stretchy mozzarella.
- **Ripening box:** This is a plastic box with a sealable lid in which cheeses are ripened. It is used to create a humid atmosphere around the cheese.

WARMING & RIPENING MILK

Milk is the key ingredient in making cheese. We buy fresh local milk from cows, goats and ewes (see pages 18–20 for more details of the fat levels in different milks and their suitability for making cheese). Probably the most important step in the cheese-making process is warming and ripening the milk. We remove the milk from the refrigerator at least an hour before starting. Then the aim is to warm the milk very gradually so that the proteins are not destroyed.

In some recipes, the milk is heated directly in a sterilized pan on the stove. In others, the milk is heated indirectly and therefore more slowly, using a water bath or double boiler. We use a thermostatically controlled electric soup kettle for the job but there are other ways of doing it. These options are described in more detail on pages 12–14.

Once the milk has been heated slowly to the temperature specified in the recipe, it is time to add the bacterial culture or the rennet to sour the milk and separate it into curds and whey. After this, the milk has to be kept at a constant temperature for a period of time to encourage the culture to develop. We again use a thermostatically controlled soup kettle to maintain the temperature, but the pot of milk could also be wrapped in a thick towel to prevent the heat escaping. Another option is a Dutch oven, a heavy cast iron pot with a ceramic lining and lid, which will also retain the heat well and prevent the milk cooling too quickly.

THE CLEAN BREAK TEST

As the rennet or bacterial culture sours the milk, it will separate into solid curds and liquid whey. In some recipes the curds are simply spooned into a colander to drain, in others the curds are cut into even pieces and drained in a mould. The test to indicate if the curds are ready to be cut is known as a clean break. Insert a knife or your finger into the curd at a slight angle. The edge of the curd should break cleanly with a sharp rather than a soft edge and the gap should fill with whey. If the cut leaves your curds messy and soft-edged, cover again and leave for another 10–15 minutes. If the curd makes a clean break, it is ready for cutting.

CUTTING THE CURDS

The size of the pieces into which you cut the curd will affect the moisture content of the resulting cheese. Large slices of curd will retain whey and make the cheese soft, while smaller pieces will result in a drier cheese. We use a palette knife for cutting the curd, but you can buy curd-cutting tools for the job. Start by making a series of evenly spaced vertical parallel cuts through the curd across the pan from the surface to the bottom, running the blade in smooth, swift lines. Then rotate the pan by a quarter turn and repeat so that you have a checked pattern. Finally, make four diagonal cuts down through the curd at an angle of 45°. Stir gently, then cut any large curds to match the rest.

DRAINING & MOULDING

Once the curds are ready to shape into a recognizable cheese, the real fun begins. The curds first have to be drained to remove some of the whey. This is done in one of three different ways. The first is to line a colander with cheesecloth and ladle the curds into it to drain. The second is to place the curds in

Cut curds with confidence, just go for it!

a draining sack or piece of cheesecloth and hang them over a bucket to drain, while the third is to transfer the curds directly to a cheese mould lined with cheesecloth.

PRESSING

Many recipes will call for you to apply weight to press the cheese and expel any remaining whey; this is common for hard cheeses. Pressing is a simple method that is easiest done in a special cheese press, but can be improvised with heavy bottles of water, cans of food or even dumbbell weights. Follow the instructions in the recipe and leave your cheese on a rack over a tray for best results.

ADDING SALT

Salt is a key ingredient in cheese, and not just to add flavour. The salt serves an important purpose in the formation of a rind to protect the cheese from unwanted bacteria. There are two ways to use salt and sometimes both methods are called for. The first is dry-salting the cheese before or after pressing and shaping. This involves sprinkling the curds with salt, which draws out the moisture from inside the cheese and allows it to evaporate. This process helps to form a dry rind and makes hard cheeses feel firmer.

The second method is to brine the cheese after pressing and shaping, by immersing it in a solution of salt and sterilized water. This serves the same job and can even be a way to add flavour to the cheese. We find that brining is an excellent way to control the addition of salt as you are aware of exactly how much salt is dissolved in the brine and you can leave the cheese in it for as little or as much time as you like.

MAKING A BRINE

Brines are classed according to how much salt they contain. For example, a medium brine contains 15 per cent salt, which is 150g (5oz) of salt per 1 litre (1¾ pints) of water. To make a brine, heat the sterilized water in a pan, add the salt and stir until dissolved. Allow to cool, then chill in the refrigerator before using.

SALT CONTENT FOR DIFFERENT BRINES

BRINE	% SALT BY WEIGHT	USES
Light brine	10%	Flavours soft, stretchy cheeses like mozzarella
Medium brine	15%	Used for storing Feta-style cheese after a short time curing
Heavy brine	20%	Adds a strong salty flavour and preserves cheeses
Saturated brine	20–25%	Use when making hard cheeses to draw in salt and draw out moisture; also helps to develop a rind

Most cheeses should be chilled to the same temperature as the brine before going into the solution, with the exception of Feta-style cheeses and Gouda-style cheeses. Leave the cheese in the brine for the length of time specified in the instructions for making each cheese. If you taste your cheese after brining and it is too salty, simply soak the cheese in clean water for 1–2 hours, then drain and pat dry before eating.

DRYING & AGEING

Drying is an important process for forming a rind on a hard cheese, and for making soft cheese hold its shape. The cheese is left uncovered in a well-ventilated area free from insects and this vital stage helps to mature it. Next, many cheeses must be ripened or aged. We find that this is the most tricky stage for the home cheese-maker to perfect, but it is perfectly achievable if you are attentive.

MAKING A RIPENING BOX

We use large plastic food-grade boxes as ripening boxes and place the cheese inside on a wire rack, sitting on a square of cheese matting. The box itself should be twice as large as the cheese to allow good air ventilation. Keep the lid of the box ajar for the first couple of days, then seal the box. Open once a day and check the cheese. Sprinkle a little salt on the surface of the cheese to keep the cheese dry but the air moist. Pat the cheese dry if necessary and take time to appreciate its progress.

When making semi-soft cheeses, such as Brie or Camembert-type cheeses, the humidity levels need to be kept high in the ripening box to encourage the mould to grow on the outside of the cheese and form a rind. Humidity can be measured using a simple device called a hygrometer, but we tend to gauge it by observing the growth of the bloom. If the mould is slow to grow, place a sheet of kitchen paper dipped in water in the bottom of the box, or a small natural sponge sitting in a bowl of water. If the mould grows very quickly, reduce the humidity in the box by removing the wet paper or sponge.

If you are making a hard cheese, you will need to remain vigilant during ripening to ensure that any unwanted bacterial growth is removed from the surface of the cheese. Wipe off any unpleasant-looking mould with a piece of cheesecloth dipped in a solution of vinegar and water. Then pat the cheese dry and continue to age.

If you are making big cheeses you may want to use a cheese iron to take a sample and decide when it is ready to eat. Alternatively, simply wait for the time specified in the instructions.

METHOD #6

COTTAGE CHEESE

For many of us today, we associate cottage cheese with dieting as it is often made with skimmed milk and is therefore lower in fat than other cheeses. We love the simplicity of making our own and it never fails to disappoint. The moist curds remain loose and are suspended in a creamy coating of whey. The mild taste is a blank canvas to which to add extra flavours, in the form of chopped chives, black pepper, cured ham or even chopped fruit.

PREPARING

We use a commercial starter and rennet to make cottage cheese. You can leave out the rennet and allow the milk to become acidic naturally over 12–24 hours, but we like to speed up the process.

If you want to make a rich cottage cheese, use whole milk and a little cream, otherwise use skimmed milk. Don't forget to sterilize your equipment before starting (see page 14).

MAKING

Heat the milk and cream slowly in a water bath or soup kettle (see pages 12–14), then add the starter and rennet and cover and keep warm while the curds and whey separate. Cut the curds into cubes (see page 73), then heat again to cook the curds and release more whey.

Drain off the whey in a cheesecloth-lined colander. The curds will appear shrivelled and may stick together a bit, but they can be separated again later. Tie up the corners of the cheesecloth to form a bag and hang it up to release most of the remaining moisture.

STORING

Store in the refrigerator in a sterilized tub for up to a week. Cottage cheese doesn't freeze well and is best enjoyed fresh.

COTTAGE CHEESE

Makes about 250g (8oz)

5 litres (8 pints) whole cows' milk

2 tablespoons double cream (optional)

⅛ teaspoon mesophilic starter

8–10 drops of rennet, mixed with 1 tablespoon sterilized water

salt

To make cottage cheese, follow the instructions above and opposite.

HOW TO MAKE COTTAGE CHEESE

Heat the milk and cream slowly in a water bath until it reaches 28–30°C (82–86°F). Turn off the heat and sprinkle the starter over the surface. Leave for 5 minutes, then stir in gently using a whisk.

Add the rennet, stir thoroughly, then cover and leave in a warm place, wrapped in a thick towel, for 5–6 hours. Cut the curds into 1cm (½ inch) cubes.

Heat again slowly over a period of 2 hours until it reaches 45°C (113°F), to firm up the curds. Stir every 5–10 minutes.

Transfer the curds to a cheesecloth-lined colander and drain for 30 minutes, then hang up by the corners of the cloth until the dripping all but stops. Season and transfer to a tub.

For many people cottage cheese has a comforting quality and a homely feel-good factor. This breakfast dish offers the perfect wake-up call to start the day in a hearty way. For an easy variation, replace the pancetta and chervil with strips of smoked salmon, finely grated lemon zest and fresh dill.

SERVES 2

1 tablespoon olive oil

100g (3½oz) pancetta, diced

200g (7oz) cottage cheese

2 tablespoons chopped fresh chervil, plus extra to garnish

2 English muffins, split and toasted

butter, for spreading

2 teaspoons cider vinegar

sea salt flakes and freshly ground black pepper

baby spinach and sprouted seed salad, to serve

ENGLISH MUFFINS WITH COTTAGE CHEESE, PANCETTA & CHERVIL

Heat the oil in a frying pan, add the pancetta and cook until golden and crisp. Mix the pancetta with the cottage cheese and chervil. Butter the muffins generously, arrange on 2 serving plates and top with the cottage cheese.

Pour the vinegar into the still-hot frying pan and stir well to deglaze the pan. Arrange some baby spinach leaves and sprouted seeds on the plates and drizzle with the dressing in the frying pan. Season with sea salt flakes and black pepper, garnish with chervil sprigs and serve immediately.

Ricotta curds are very fine

METHOD #7

RICOTTA-STYLE CHEESE

The word ricotta comes from the Italian for 're-cooked' as it was traditionally made from large batches of whey left over from making other cheeses. The temperature and acidity of the whey were increased until further curds formed. We rarely have that much whey in the house, so we make ricotta using cows' milk and a little double cream if we want a rich version. This cheese is excellent as a lower-fat substitute for mascarpone, and can be used in a wide range of pasta dishes.

MAKING

Ricotta is made by heating milk or whey and adding citric acid to make the curds form. When heating the milk, stir constantly with a rubber spatula to distribute the heat and avoid burning or scalding the curds that form on the edges of the pan. At the end of the cooking time, don't scrape off any scalded curds which stick to the pan as they may have a less pleasant taste and ruin your ricotta.

The curds that form are very fine, so you need to use very fine cheesecloth, or use a triple layer of standard cheesecloth and drain the cheese in a sieve rather than a colander for extra support. After 15 minutes in the sieve, pull the corners of the cheesecloth up together to make a draining sack and hang over a bowl in the refrigerator for 2–4 hours, depending on how moist you like your ricotta.

STORING

Transfer the ricotta to a sealed container in the refrigerator and use within 1–2 weeks.

Salting the curds will extend the shelf-life but can overpower the delicate flavour and negates the healthier option.

NOW TRY: GOATS' RICOTTA

Follow the instructions for cows' milk, but use twice the quantity of citric acid to help with coagulation. The curds will be even softer, so add another layer of cheesecloth when draining to prevent losing the delicate curds.

NOW TRY: WHEY CHEESE

To try this you'll need a huge amount of fresh whey. For approximately 150g (5oz) of ricotta, you will need to start with about 23 litres (5 gallons) of whey that has been treated with a starter while making another cheese. Start by leaving the whey at room temperature overnight to allow the leftover bacteria in the whey to convert the remaining sugars into lactic acid and make the milk acidic. Then follow the instructions for heating and draining to make the ricotta.

HOW TO MAKE RICOTTA-STYLE CHEESE

1

2

Heat the milk, cream, citric acid and the salt slowly in a water bath or soup kettle over a period of 15–20 minutes until it reaches 83–85°C (181–185°F).

When the curds start to float to the surface and the whey develops a yellow-green tinge, turn off the heat and allow to stand, undisturbed, for 10–15 minutes.

3

Transfer the curds to a sieve lined with 3 layers of cheesecloth and drain for 15 minutes, then hang up by the corners of the cloth in the refrigerator for 2–4 hours.

RICOTTA-STYLE CHEESE

Makes about 250g (8oz)

5 litres (8 pints) whole cows'
milk
....
100ml (3½fl oz) double cream
(optional)
....
2 teaspoons citric acid powder
....
1 teaspoon salt
....

To make ricotta-style cheese, follow the instructions above and opposite.

Ricotta is an excellent accompaniment to pasta and benefits from being combined with robust flavours. Our version of cannelloni pairs the ricotta with squash and sage rather than the usual spinach. Our rationale is that you need to grow a lot of spinach to fill the pasta tubes, but one butternut squash should provide enough filling for at least two meals.

SERVES 4

4 tablespoons olive oil

1 garlic clove, chopped

a handful of chopped celery

1 teaspoon chopped fresh parsley stems

½ carrot, peeled and grated

400g (13oz) can chopped tomatoes

salt and freshly ground black pepper

200g (7oz) peeled butternut squash, finely diced

2 shallots, sliced

6-8 fresh sage leaves, shredded

400g (13oz) ricotta-style cheese

1 egg, beaten

20 cannelloni tubes

FOR THE BECHAMEL SAUCE

50g (2oz) butter

1 garlic clove, peeled

50g (2oz) plain flour

500ml (17fl oz) milk

1 tablespoon grated Parmesan cheese

a pinch of grated nutmeg

RICOTTA & SQUASH CANNELLONI

Heat half the oil in a pan over a medium heat, add the garlic, celery, parsley stems and carrot and fry for 2–3 minutes until softened. Add the tomatoes, season to taste and bring to the boil. Reduce the heat and simmer for 15–20 minutes, then transfer to a shallow ovenproof dish into which the cannelloni tubes will fit in a single layer.

For the bechamel sauce, melt the butter in a pan over a medium heat, add the garlic, then gradually stir in the flour. Add the milk, a little at a time, and continue cooking and stirring until the sauce thickens. Remove the garlic, season to taste and stir in the Parmesan and nutmeg.

Heat the remaining oil in a frying pan and add the squash, shallots and half the sage. Cook for 5–10 minutes or until starting to caramelize, then season to taste and allow to cool.

Preheat the oven to 200°C (400°F), Gas Mark 6. Mix the squash with the ricotta and the beaten egg, season and spoon the mixture into the pasta tubes. Lay the stuffed tubes in the dish on top of the tomato sauce, then cover with the bechamel sauce and sprinkle with the remaining sage leaves. Cook in the oven for 40 minutes, or until the pasta is tender and the sauce is bubbling.

A black pepper cream cheese roule

METHOD #8

CREAM CHEESE

Cream cheese is very easy to make and perfect for home production. It is an excellent carrier of flavours when used in cooking, or can be pressed into moulds to make an impressive-looking cheese with a distinctive shape. The key in its production is to ripen the milk slowly to provide that creamy texture you know and love.

PREPARING

For guaranteed richness, make the cream cheese with half milk and half cream. However, if you can get a good batch of rich milk with a high cream content, you can leave out the cream and make the cheese with just milk. In which case, follow the instructions opposite but use 5 litres (8 pints) of milk, ⅛ teaspoon of mesophilic starter and 4–6 drops of rennet, and heat the milk to just 25°C (77°F). Don't forget to sterilize your equipment before starting (see page 14).

MAKING

Cream cheese is made by heating the milk and cream, then adding a starter culture to separate the curds and whey. The curds are then drained in a colander until they are the right texture.

The key to making traditional cream cheese with a creamy texture and real flavour is to leave plenty of time for the milk to mature. The curds will form in under an hour, and could be drained at that stage, but if they are left overnight they develop their special taste. The longer you leave the curds draining the firmer the cheese will become.

SHAPING

If you want to shape the cream cheese, pack into an oiled plastic mould and chill in the refrigerator for 2–3 hours to set. Dip the mould in warm water to loosen the cheese before turning out and dressing with sesame seeds, pink peppercorns or finely chopped herbs. You can use household objects like mugs, old yoghurt pots and even old jelly moulds to shape the cheese. Be creative and serve your classic cream cheese in an original way.

STORING

Press the cheese into an airtight container or a mould and store in the refrigerator for up to 2 weeks. Removing air gaps is vital to extend the shelf-life of your cream cheese.

NOW TRY: ROULE

Spread the cream cheese in an even layer on a piece of clingfilm, then sprinkle with chopped herbs, finely chopped garlic, grated horseradish or cracked black pepper. Roll up the cheese carefully to form a long sausage shape, wrap in the clingfilm and chill until ready to serve. Serve sliced into rounds on a warm baguette.

HOW TO MAKE CREAM CHEESE

CLASSIC CREAM CHEESE

Makes about 250g (8oz)

1 litre (1¾ pints) whole cows' milk

1 litre (1¾ pints) double cream

¼ teaspoon mesophilic starter

3 drops of rennet, mixed with 1 tablespoon sterilized water

2 drops of calcium chloride, mixed with 1 tablespoon sterilized water

salt

To make cream cheese, follow the instructions below and opposite.

Heat the milk and cream slowly in a water bath over a period of 15–20 minutes until it reaches 40°C (104°F). Turn off the heat and allow to cool to 30°C (86°F).

Sprinkle the starter over the surface and leave for 5 minutes. Stir in the starter gently using a whisk, then add the rennet and calcium chloride.

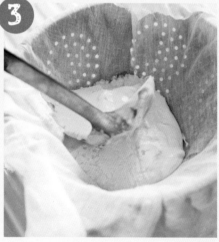

Cover and leave in a warm place, wrapped in a thick towel, for 12 hours. Transfer to a cheesecloth-lined colander and drain for 6–8 hours, then season to taste.

It is hard to not smile when you're eating this dessert, partly due to the sentimental heart shape, and partly because of the great taste. If you want to try something different, add a selection of chopped fruit or nuts to the cheese mixture before putting it in the moulds. You will need six heart-shaped moulds with drainage holes, or a simple sieve to shape the dessert.

SERVES 6

200g (7oz) caster sugar

350g (11½oz) cream cheese

600ml (1 pint) double cream

2 teaspoons vanilla extract

fresh mint leaves, to decorate

FOR THE RASPBERRY COULIS

1 tablespoon Grand Marnier

175g (6oz) raspberries, plus extra to decorate

50g (2oz) caster sugar

COEURS À LA CRÈME

Beat the sugar and cream cheese together in a bowl, then add the cream and vanilla and beat by hand or with a hand-held electric whisk until it forms soft peaks. Line 6 heart-shaped moulds with cheesecloth, divide the mixture between them and wrap the loose edges of the cheesecloth over the top. Alternatively, pour the mixture into a sieve lined with cheesecloth and placed over a bowl. Place on a tray and leave in the refrigerator overnight.

To make the raspberry coulis, place all the ingredients in a pan and place over a medium heat. Bring to the boil, then lower the heat and simmer for 3 minutes. Allow to cool, then press through a fine sieve and divide between 6 plates or bowls. Unwrap the cheese mixture and arrange on top of the coulis. Serve decorated with a few fresh raspberries and mint leaves.

Gently does it...

Choux pastry takes a little time to prepare but makes a lovely crisp contrast to a creamy filling. This recipe can be adapted to suit your mood as the cream cheese can be flavoured with different ingredients. Here we use crab meat, asparagus and tarragon. The tarragon can be replaced with finely chopped fresh red chilli and fresh ginger, or some finely grated lemon zest if you prefer.

SERVES 8

125g (4oz) cream cheese

100g (3½oz) white crab meat

50g (2oz) asparagus tips, steamed, cooled and chopped

1 teaspoon chopped fresh tarragon

salt and freshly ground black pepper

30g (1¼ oz) butter, plus extra for greasing

75ml (3fl oz) water

75ml (3fl oz) whole cows' or goats' milk

75g (3oz) plain flour

2 eggs, beaten

lemon wedges, to serve

CRAB CHOUX POTS

Beat the cream cheese until it becomes light and fluffy, then add the crab meat, asparagus and tarragon and season to taste. Set aside.

Preheat the oven to 200°C (400°F), Gas Mark 6, and grease 8 ovenproof ramekins. Place the water, milk and butter in a pan, bring to the boil and then remove from the heat. Add the flour and mix quickly to combine, then return to the heat and cook until the mixture thickens. Remove from the heat and beat in the eggs a little at a time, beating vigorously until the mixture is smooth and glossy.

Transfer the choux pastry to a piping bag and pipe a ring of pastry around the base of each ramekin. Repeat to make a double ring around each ramekin, then spoon the cheese mixture into the ramekins to fill the centres. Cook in the oven for 10–15 minutes until the pastry is puffed and golden and the filling is bubbling. Serve immediately with lemon wedges.

METHOD #9

MASCARPONE-STYLE CHEESE

Mascarpone is a rich, fresh cream cheese that is probably best known as the basis for a number of desserts, including cheesecakes and tiramisu. If you have a sweet tooth this simple cheese is extremely useful, but it can also be used in savoury dishes such as risotto, lasagne and cannelloni to add a creamy richness.

MAKING

The cream has to be heated very gently when making mascarpone, so use a water bath, double boiler or soup kettle (see page 12).

STORING

It can be kept in an airtight container in the refrigerator for up to a week. Salting the finished cheese will add some storage time.

HOW TO MAKE MASCARPONE-STYLE CHEESE

Heat 1 litre (1¾ pints) of double cream slowly in a water bath, double boiler or soup kettle until it reaches 85°C (185°F).

Mix ¼ teaspoon of citric acid powder with 2 tablespoons of sterilized water, then pour the mixture into the cream.

Gently stir the cream for 10 minutes until fine curds form. If they do not form, add another batch of citric acid and water and stir for another 10 minutes.

Transfer the mixture to a cheesecloth-lined colander and drain for 90 minutes.

Tie the corners of the cheesecloth together to form a bag and remove from the colander.

Hang the bag over a bowl in the refrigerator and leave to drain for at least 8 hours until the dripping stops.

A baked cheesecake has a very different texture from the light fluffy varieties that are set with gelatine. This one has a rich, creamy and smooth filling, which is studded with juicy blueberries.

SERVES 6

150g (5oz) butter, softened, plus extra for greasing

100g (3½oz) caster sugar

½ teaspoon vanilla extract

3 eggs, separated

4 tablespoons lemon juice

4 tablespoons double cream

625g (1¼lb) mascarpone-style cheese, softened

100g (3½oz) blueberries

icing sugar, for dusting

FOR THE BASE

175g (6oz) digestive biscuits

65g (2½oz) butter, melted

BAKED BLUEBERRY CHEESECAKE

Preheat the oven to 180°C (350°F), Gas Mark 4. Grease a 20cm (8 inch) springform cake tin and line the base with greaseproof paper.

To make the base, place the digestive biscuits in a plastic bag and crush with a rolling pin to form fine crumbs. Transfer to a bowl, stir in the melted butter and mix well. Spoon the mixture into the tin and press down firmly with the back of a spoon to make an even layer. Chill in the refrigerator.

Cream the butter with the sugar and vanilla until fluffy, then beat in the egg yolks and lemon juice. Add the cream and mascarpone and beat until smooth.

Whisk the egg whites until just stiff, then mix about one-third into the cheese mixture. Carefully fold in the remaining egg whites and the blueberries using a metal spoon. Pour the mixture on to the biscuit base and level the surface. Place the tin on a baking sheet and cook in the oven for 1 hour. Turn off the heat and leave the cheesecake in the oven to cool, leaving the door slightly ajar.

Carefully remove the cheesecake from the tin and serve dusted with icing sugar.

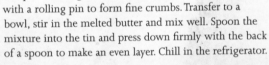

the first slice is always the most difficult

Tiramisu has been popular in our household for years. Our version uses fried doughnuts instead of the traditional sponge fingers, and the doughnuts are filled with our creamy and rich homemade mascarpone. You need a little finesse to pipe the filling into the light doughnuts, but this is a winning team that celebrates this Italian cream cheese.

MAKES 16

125g (4oz) mascarpone-style cheese

2 tablespoons icing sugar

1 shot of espresso coffee, cooled

250g (8oz) plain flour, plus extra for dusting

100ml (3½fl oz) milk

50g (2oz) butter, softened

1 large egg, beaten

1 teaspoon fast-action dried yeast

a pinch of salt

vegetable oil, for greasing and frying

FOR DUSTING

50g (2oz) granulated sugar

a pinch of instant coffee powder

a pinch of ground cinnamon

a pinch of cocoa powder

TIRAMISU DOUGHNUTS

Make the filling by mixing the mascarpone with the icing sugar, then swirling through the cooled coffee. Transfer to a piping bag fitted with a doughnut-filling nozzle and set aside. Place all the dusting ingredients in a paper bag and shake to mix, then set aside.

Place the flour, milk, butter, egg, yeast and salt in a mixing bowl and beat to form a dough. Place the dough on a lightly floured work surface and knead for 5–10 minutes until smooth and glossy. Transfer to a lightly oiled bowl, cover with a tea towel and leave to rise in a warm place for 30–40 minutes.

Divide the dough into 16 pieces, roll into neat balls and space well apart on a lightly oiled baking sheet. Cover with oiled clingfilm and leave to prove in a warm place until doubled in size.

Heat some vegetable oil to 160°C (325°F) in a large pan or deep-fryer. Place 2 or 3 doughnuts in the pan and cook until golden underneath, then turn over and deep-fry the other sides until golden. Transfer to a plate lined with kitchen paper, then cook the remaining doughnuts in the same way and allow to cool.

Preheat the oven to 200°C (400°F), Gas Mark 6. Pipe the filling into the doughnuts, then place them on a baking sheet and cook in the oven for 30 seconds. Transfer to the paper bag with the dusting ingredients, a few at a time, and shake well to coat.

Of all the soft cheeses in the world, this is probably the most famous. The smooth texture and iconic flavour are perfectly balanced, giving this cheese an elegance in its simplicity. Special goats' cheese starter cultures, containing a balance of rennet and mesophilic culture, are now readily available to capture the subtleties of a good goats' cheese and make it easy to create at home.

MAKES ABOUT 250G (8OZ)

5 litres (8 pints) whole goats' milk

⅛ teaspoon chèvre starter

FRESH GOATS' CHEESE

Heat the milk slowly in a water bath until it reaches 30°C (86°F). Turn off the heat and sprinkle the starter over the surface. Leave for 5 minutes, then stir in gently using a whisk. Cover and leave to cool, then stand at room temperature for 12–14 hours for the curds and whey to separate.

Transfer the curds to a cheesecloth-lined colander and drain for 15–20 minutes. Then either hang up by the corners of the cloth or transfer to cheesecloth-lined moulds with drainage holes, and leave to drain at room temperature for another 12 hours. If using moulds, turn the cheeses after 6 hours.

Keep the cheese in a sealed container in the refrigerator and consume within a week.

The cheese can be sprinkled with spices and fresh or dried herbs before serving. Some good combinations include honey and paprika, chopped tarragon, chervil and rose petals, pink peppercorns and toasted fennel seeds, and smoked salt, dill and lemon zest. A selection of all these different flavours makes a very impressive cheese board.

The idea of making soufflés strikes fear into many home cooks, but it isn't as difficult or as complicated as you may think. The key is a light and fluffy mixture - plus staying patient and not opening the oven door to peek before they are ready. These soufflés are delicious served with a rocket salad.

SERVES 6

50g (2oz) butter, softened, plus extra for greasing

50g (2oz) plain flour, plus extra for dusting

200ml (7fl oz) milk

75g (3oz) fresh goats' cheese

a pinch of grated nutmeg

4 eggs, separated

GOATS' CHEESE SOUFFLÉS

Preheat the oven to 200°C (400°F), Gas Mark 6. Grease 6 ovenproof ramekins and dust them with flour. Heat the milk in a small pan over a medium heat, add the cheese and nutmeg and stir until melted, removing the pan from the heat before it boils.

Cream the butter with the flour in a mixing bowl until well mixed, then beat in the egg yolks. Slowly pour in the warm milk, gradually beating until the mixture is smooth and glossy.

Whisk the egg whites until they form soft peaks, then gently fold into the cheese with a metal spoon, taking care not to lose any of the air in the mixture. Spoon the batter into the prepared ramekins and cook in the oven for 15 minutes. Do not open the oven door during cooking as the loss of heat could cause the rising soufflés to collapse. Serve immediately.

METHOD #10

FETA-STYLE CHEESE

This is our twist on the well-known crumbly white cheese that made an impression on us years ago when enjoying a holiday in Greece. 'Feta' is now a legally protected name that can only be used to describe a specific type of cheese made in Greece. That said, there are many variations made elsewhere, all with slightly different textures and ingredients. Our version uses both a dry salt cure and a brining process to add flavour and preserve the cheese for longer. We also store our cheese in olive oil after brining to add more flavour — this is a great shortcut to the perfect Greek salad.

PREPARING

This crumbly brined cheese can be made with goats' milk or ewes' milk, depending on what you can find available. The method is interchangeable with both, or indeed a mixture of the two.

If you want your cheese to have a traditional block shape, you can buy a special straight-sided cheese mould. Alternatively, make your own mould using an old plastic food container. Drill or puncture a series of small holes in the sides and base of the container to allow the whey to drain away.

MAKING

Buttermilk is used to provide the culture to sour the milk. After gentle warming, the milk has to be kept at a constant temperature for more than 2 hours in all. This is where a thermostatically controlled soup kettle is very useful. If you don't have one, wrap the pan in

a thick towel and keep it in a warm place. The resulting curds are cut into cubes (see page 73), and drained in a colander or packed into a mould to drain. The drained cheese is

then cut into cubes and dry cured with salt to draw out more of the moisture.

The cheese is ready to eat after the dry curing stage, but it can be kept in brine to preserve it for longer. See page 74 for details of making a brine. Use a light brine if you are going to eat the cheese fairly quickly, or a medium brine if you want the cheese to last 2–3 months.

STORING

If the cheese is dry cured with salt, then stored in a medium brine, it should stay edible for 2–3 months. If you miss out the salting stage and place the cheese straight into a light brine, consume within 2–3 weeks.

NOW TRY: PRESERVING IN OIL

The cheese can be stored in olive oil instead of brine after dry curing. The oil itself adds flavour to the cheese, but you could also add roasted red peppers, garlic, jalapeños, dried herbs or spices to the oil. Marinate the cheese in the oil for a few days, then spread on toast or use the cubes of cheese and their oil as an instant dressing for a salad. Cheese that has been marinated in olive oil with other ingredients should be consumed within 2–3 weeks.

FETA-STYLE CHEESE

Makes 300–400g (10–13oz)

5 litres (8 pints) whole goats' milk

500ml (17fl oz) buttermilk

6-8 drops of rennet, mixed with 1 tablespoon sterilized water

4 tablespoons sea salt flakes

1 litre (1¾ pints) medium brine (see page 74)

To make Feta-style cheese, follow the instructions above and overleaf.

HOW TO MAKE FETA-STYLE CHEESE

1

Heat the milk slowly in a water bath over a period of 15–20 minutes until it reaches 32°C (90°F). Add the buttermilk and keep at a constant temperature for 1 hour.

2

Add the rennet, stir for 2 minutes, then leave for another hour. Cut the curds into 1cm (½ inch) cubes (see page 73) and leave undisturbed for 15 minutes, still at 32°C (90°F).

5

Remove the cheese from the moulds and turn it over every hour for a uniform shape.

6

Cut the cheese into 1–2.5cm (½–1 inch) cubes and sprinkle evenly with sea salt. Cover with an upturned bowl and keep in the refrigerator for 5 days.

Transfer the curds to a cheesecloth-lined colander and drain for 1 hour.

If you have them, pack the curds into moulds lined with cheesecloth and leave to drain for 4 hours. Alternatively, leave for another 4 hours in the colander.

Sprinkle with more salt every day or two, turning the cubes over and pouring off any liquid. Or, instead of curing with dry salt, soak the cheese in a light brine.

If storing the cheese for any length of time, transfer it to an airtight container, cover the cheese with a medium brine solution and store in the refrigerator.

We've been enjoying this classic dish for years and somehow it still surprises us. The balance of cheese, spinach and nutmeg is never the same, no matter how often we cook it. Fortunately we like surprises and the subtleties of a slightly larger pinch of nutmeg or a more potent cheese makes this recipe a culinary improvisation every time.

SERVES 4

50g (2oz) butter, plus extra for greasing

2 onions, sliced

2 garlic cloves, chopped

500g (1lb) spinach, chopped

2 eggs, beaten

200g (7oz) Feta-style cheese, crumbled

1 tablespoon chopped fresh parsley

a pinch of grated nutmeg

salt and freshly ground black pepper

4 large sheets of filo pastry

FETA FILO ROLLS

Melt half the butter in a pan over a low heat, add the onions and garlic and cook gently for 5–10 minutes until tender. Add the spinach and cook until wilted, then transfer the vegetables to a mixing bowl, leaving any liquid behind in the pan.

Mix the beaten eggs with the cheese, parsley and nutmeg, then stir into the spinach mixture and season to taste. Preheat the oven to 180°C (350°F), Gas Mark 4. Grease a baking sheet and melt the remaining butter.

Lay a sheet of pastry on the work surface and spoon one-quarter of the filling along one edge. Roll up the pastry to enclose the filling, brush with melted butter and place on the prepared baking sheet. Repeat with the remaining pastry and filling. Cook in the oven for 20 minutes until crisp and golden. Serve hot or cold.

Carefully roll up each parcel

HALLOUMI-STYLE CHEESE

When we first made a halloumi-style cheese, we were amazed at the simplicity of the process. We had always assumed that the secret technique was safe-guarded by Cypriot goat-herders and shrouded in mountain mystery. Halloumi has become incredibly popular due to its unique texture and flexibility as an ingredient. This cheese has a structure that makes it ideal for cooking, and the salty taste and fresh tang are robust enough to be served with spices and other strong flavours. There is some debate over how to cook it, but we opt for a little oil and aromatic marinades with plenty of herbs.

PREPARING

Halloumi-style cheese doesn't require a starter culture; all you need is milk, rennet and salt. Be sure to sterilize all your equipment before use, even the jars in which you are going to store the finished cheese.

MAKING

Halloumi-style cheese is made by separating the curds from the whey using rennet. The curds are drained, pressed and cut into blocks, then the blocks of cheese are cooked in the reserved whey. They are then air-dried and stored in whey or brine until ready to serve.

PRESSING

Pressing the cheese can be done with a rectangular cheese mould and a special cheese press, or in a more improvised fashion. The cheese needs to be wrapped in cheesecloth and placed in a perforated container so the whey can drain off when the cheese is pressed. Place a board or other flat object on top of the cheese, then apply weights in the form of bottles of water, heavy cans of food or weights from dumbbells.

AIR DRYING

After cooking the blocks of cheese in the whey, it must be allowed to dry before storing. This part of the process is very simple but, like all stages of cheese-making, requires attention to detail. Place the blocks or cubes of cheese on a piece of cheese matting and sprinkle with salt to draw out the remaining moisture. Turn the cheese every 10–15 minutes so it dries evenly. A cheese safe is a good place for air drying as it allows good ventilation, while protecting the cheese from insects. Use a piece of kitchen paper to test the surface for excess moisture and pat the cheese dry before storage.

STORING

Halloumi-style cheese stores very well in the refrigerator, making it the perfect cheese to make in large quantities to maximize the time and effort involved. Jam jars are a good size for storing the cheese. If the cheese is stored in whey, it should be consumed within 2–5 days. If it is stored in brine, it will keep for up to 2 months.

COOKING

Halloumi-style cheeses are usually cooked before being eaten. Slice the cheese thickly, then barbecue, grill or pan-fry it until golden and crusty on the outside and soft and melted inside.

NOW TRY: FLAVOURING

Halloumi and other similar cheeses from the western Mediterranean are flavoured with herbs to complement the subtle tang of the goats' milk and the salty brine. Sprinkle a mixture of dried mint, oregano, thyme or fennel over the draining curds or into the whey during cooking. Any flavour added at this stage can only add to the enjoyment of the cheese on your plate.

HALLOUMI-STYLE CHEESE

Makes 1kg (2lb)

10 litres (16 pints) whole goats' or ewes' milk

15 drops of rennet, mixed with 1 tablespoon sterilized water

2 teaspoons salt

2.5 litres (4 pints) medium brine solution (see page 73) (optional)

To make halloumi-style cheese, follow the instructions above and overleaf.

HOW TO MAKE HALLOUMI-STYLE CHEESE

Heat the milk slowly in a water bath to 25°C (77°F), add the rennet and keep at a constant temperature for 1 hour.

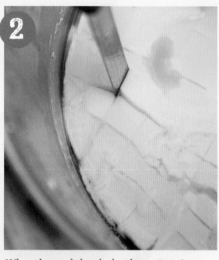

When the curds break cleanly, cut into 1cm (½ inch) cubes. Leave to rest for 5–10 minutes in the pan.

Heat the reserved whey in a pan over a period of 30 minutes to 87°C (189°F).

Cut the curds into 75–100g (3–3½oz) blocks and cook in the whey for 30–40 minutes, or until they float to the surface.

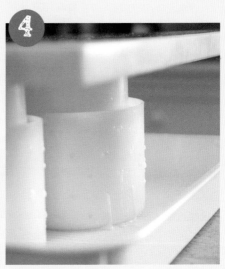

Transfer the curds to a cheesecloth-lined colander. Sprinkle with half the salt and drain for 15 minutes. Reserve the whey, placing it in the refrigerator for later use.

Transfer the curds to cheese moulds or other straight-sided perforated containers lined with cheesecloth and press with 4kg (8lb) for 3 hours.

Remove the cheese from the whey and place on a sterilized board, sprinkle with the remaining salt and leave to air dry for 1 hour, turning occasionally.

Pat dry and store in an airtight container in a medium brine or the reserved whey.

Halloumi is a cheese that can take on bold flavours. This hearty breakfast plays on the salty quality of halloumi and tempers the squeaky texture of the cheese by grilling the outside into caramelized cubes. The spinach helps to cut through the rich cheese, and a creamy poached egg balances the hint of chilli.

SERVES 2

150g (5oz) halloumi-style cheese, cubed

zest and juice of ½ a lime

1 tablespoon chopped fresh coriander

1 garlic clove, chopped

1 fresh red chilli, finely sliced

salt and freshly ground black pepper

a knob of butter

½ a red onion, finely sliced

100g (3½oz) baby spinach

1 tablespoon balsamic vinegar

a pinch of grated nutmeg

1 tablespoon sesame or vegetable oil

12 cherry tomatoes

2 bagels, split and toasted

mayonnaise, for spreading

2 eggs, lightly poached

HALLOUMI BREAKFAST BAGELS

Place the halloumi in a bowl with the lime zest and juice, coriander, garlic and chilli. Season to taste and set aside.

Heat the butter in a pan over a low heat, add the onion and cook gently for 5–10 minutes until softened. Add the spinach and cook until wilted, then add the balsamic vinegar and nutmeg and season to taste.

Meanwhile, heat the oil in a frying pan until very hot, then add the cheese and cook, turning regularly, for 3–4 minutes until golden, adding the tomatoes for the last minute of cooking.

Spread the toasted bagels with mayonnaise, then top with the spinach, followed by the cheese and tomatoes. Top each with a poached egg, season to taste and serve immediately.

Paneer is an Indian cheese with a subtle flavour and is very simple to make. The reason we like it so much is that it is robust enough in structure to fry, and stands out when cooked in a sauce-laden curry dish. We also toss our paneer in a spicy rub, then fry it in ghee for an authentic side dish to accompany an Indian meal.

SERVES 4

3 litres (5¼ pints) whole milk

4 tablespoons white vinegar

200ml (7fl oz) live natural yoghurt

ghee, for frying

FOR THE GARAM MASALA RUB

1 teaspoon cardamom seeds

1 teaspoon black peppercorns

1 teaspoon cumin seeds

1 teaspoon cloves

1 teaspoon grated nutmeg

1 cinnamon stick

a pinch of ground turmeric

SPICED PANEER

To make the paneer, heat the milk gently in a water bath until just below boiling point. Add the vinegar and yoghurt and stir well, then remove from the heat when the curds rise to the surface. Leave to stand for 15–20 minutes, then transfer the curds to a cheesecloth-lined colander and leave to drain for 10 minutes.

Tie the corners of the cheesecloth together to form a bag, then squeeze and rinse under cold running water to wash away any remaining vinegar. Place the wrapped curds on a tray or cheese mat, place a board on top and weight down with bottles of water or cans of food. This will press the curds and any remaining whey will drain off. Leave to set for 4 hours, then cut the cheese into cubes.

To make the spice rub, use a coffee grinder or pestle and mortar to crush all the ingredients to a powder. Sprinkle a heaped tablespoon of the mixture over the cubes of cheese and rub in to coat evenly.

Heat some ghee in a frying pan until hot, add the cheese and fry for 3–4 minutes, turning regularly, until golden. Serve hot. You could serve the spicy cheese with spinach for a classic *sag paneer*.

Store the leftover spice rub in an airtight jar in a cool, dark place.

balls of mozzarella floating in brine

METHOD #12

MOZZARELLA-STYLE CHEESE

The high moisture content is what makes mozzarella so good for melting on pizzas and in pasta dishes, but it is equally impressive when eaten fresh, dripping with milky whey. The Italian word *mozzare* means to tear or cut, and this method of dividing up the stretchy curds into balls is what gives our homemade version such authenticity.

Have fun and don't expect to make perfect round balls of cheese. Listen to Italian opera while stretching your curds and try not to overwork them.

PREPARING

The pH level is important when making mozzarella, so it may be worth investing in a pH meter or some indicator strips (see page 72). The more precise you are when making mozzarella, the more elastic and chewy your cheese will be.

Don't forget to sterilize your equipment before starting (see page 14).

MAKING

Mozzarella is made by souring milk with a starter culture, or by adding some live yoghurt and buttermilk to separate the curds and whey. The curds are drained in a colander, then returned to the pan and kept at a constant temperature of 38–40°C (100–104°F) for 2 hours. Use a water bath (see page 12) for this stage.

Check the pH level frequently during this time as it will start to fall. You need to catch it when it is between 4.9 and 5.2 because this

is the perfect time to stretch the cheese as it is at its most elastic.

Start by measuring the pH every 30 minutes then, when it drops below 5.5, test it every 10–15 minutes as it can fall rapidly. When the pH falls below 5.2, the curd is ready for stretching, and can be transferred to a sterilized chopping board and cut into 2.5cm (1 inch) cubes. The pH level will fall quickly, but don't panic and concentrate carefully on stretching the curd.

STRETCHING

The curds are stretched and worked until they become smooth and silky. This skill takes practice to master and, like kneading bread, there is a knack to it.

Wear heat-resistant gloves because the curds will be very hot. Start by stretching a manageable portion of curds, about one-third or one-half of the total, into a rope about 30–40cm (12–16 inches) long and then fold it over on itself. Repeat 2 or 3 times until it is smooth and glossy. The key is to dip the curd back in the hot water if it becomes too dry and cold to stretch.

While the curd is still pliable, tear it into smaller portions (about 100g/3½oz) and form into neat balls, tucking the ends in. Rotate and press the edges into the middle of the curd, repeating until you have one nice smooth side and a fairly uniform ball shape. As soon as you have shaped the curd ball, plunge it into a bowl of iced water to set.

STORING

Soak the balls of cheese in a chilled light brine (see page 73) for 6–8 hours to firm up the texture, impart a saltier flavour and keep it fresh for a few days. Make the brine with water or the reserved whey. Drain and store in the refrigerator in a sealed container, covered with water, for up to a week. Ideally, consume within 3 days to enjoy it at its best.

MOZZARELLA-STYLE CHEESE

Makes 4–5 balls

5 litres (8 pints) whole cows' milk

¼ teaspoon thermophilic starter, or 75ml (3fl oz) buttermilk and 75ml (3fl oz) live natural yoghurt

6–8 drops of rennet, mixed with 1 tablespoon sterilized water

light brine solution (see page 73)

To make mozzarella-style cheese, follow the instructions above and overleaf.

MARINATED MOZZARELLA

This simple combination of flavours infuses the cheese with both zing and a subtle depth. Try adding other Mediterranean herbs to the oil, such as rosemary or thyme, but remember to allow the flavour of the cheese to stand out. There's no point making a delicious cheese if you can't taste it through an over-infused oil.

Serves 4

2 balls of mozzarella-style cheese

1 teaspoon fennel seeds, toasted

6–8 fresh basil leaves, finely chopped

1 teaspoon dried oregano

1 teaspoon pink peppercorns

pared zest of 1 lemon

a pinch of sea salt flakes

75ml (3fl oz) olive oil

Place all the ingredients in a bowl, cover and let stand for 20–30 minutes for the flavours to mingle. Serve with air-dried ham, olives, ripe tomatoes and ciabatta.

A taste of the Mediterranean

HOW TO MAKE MOZZARELLA-STYLE CHEESE

1

Heat the milk slowly in a water bath until it reaches 30°C (86°F). Turn off the heat and stir in the buttermilk and starter or yoghurt.

2

Add the rennet and stir, then cover and leave in a warm place for 1 hour. Cut the curds and leave for 30 minutes.

5

Place the curds in a water bath, heat to 38–40°C (100–104°F) and retain at this temperature for 2 hours, turning the curds occasionally. When the pH level is 4.9–5.2, remove and cut into cubes.

6

Heat a pan of water or whey to 80°C (176°F) and add to the cheese. Alternatively, place the cheese in a bowl and microwave for 30 seconds at a time until pliable and hot to handle.

Heat slowly, stirring, over a period of 30 minutes until it reaches 40°C (104°F). Remove from the heat and stir around the edges of the pan for 5–10 minutes.

After 15 minutes, transfer the curds to a cheesecloth-lined colander and drain for 20 minutes, collecting the whey if you want to use it later.

Knead the curd into one lump and stretch it out into a long rope. Fold it over on itself a few times until smooth and silky.

Divide into portions and form into neat balls, then plunge into iced water and leave for 10 minutes. Store in brine made from water or whey, if you like.

We love cooking burgers over a grill, and a classic cheeseburger is hard to beat. However, this dish flips the burger on its head by stuffing it with a generous portion of mozzarella. The combination of intense barbecue flavour and spiced pork contrasts nicely with the pure milky cheese inside.

SERVES 4

500g (1lb) chorizo-flavoured sausagemeat

plain flour, for dusting

125g (4oz) mozzarella-style cheese, cut into 4

salt and freshly ground black pepper

1 rosemary focaccia loaf

50g (2oz) tapenade

100g (3½oz) frisée salad

olive oil vinaigrette

THE MOTHER OF ALL MOZZARELLA BURGERS

Shape the sausagemeat into 8 equal-sized patties and place on a floured work surface. Place a piece of mozzarella on 4 of the patties and top each with another patty. Press around the edges to seal the cheese inside and shape into burgers. Chill in the refrigerator for at least 30–40 minutes to firm up.

Season the burgers, then cook on a barbecue or under a preheated hot grill for 4–6 minutes on each side until cooked through.

Slice the focaccia and spread with tapenade. Dress the frisée salad with vinaigrette and arrange on 4 slices of bread, then top each with a burger. Serve immediately.

We all know that mozzarella is fantastic laid generously over a summer salad or as the ultimate topping on a pizza, but it is also delicious hidden inside the depths of a dish like arancini. This dish conceals the oozing cheese inside a fried risotto shell.

SERVES 4

2 tablespoons olive oil

250g (8oz) risotto rice

100ml (3½fl oz) dry white vermouth or white wine

a generous pinch of saffron threads

750ml (1¼pints) hot chicken stock

50g (2oz) Parmesan, grated

salt and freshly ground black pepper

125g (4oz) mozzarella-style cheese

16 fresh basil leaves

16 sun-blush tomatoes

plain flour, for dusting

2 eggs, beaten

breadcrumbs, for coating

vegetable oil, for frying

TO SERVE

chicory and radicchio salad

balsamic vinaigrette

½ a pink grapefruit, thinly sliced

ARANCINI WITH MOZZARELLA

Heat the olive oil in a pan over a medium heat, add the rice and cook, stirring, for 1–2 minutes. Add the vermouth or wine and bubble until reduced by half, then add the saffron, followed by a ladleful of hot stock. Cook, stirring continuously, until the stock has all but been absorbed, then add another ladleful. Continue cooking and stirring, adding more stock when necessary, for 15–20 minutes, until the rice is tender. Add the Parmesan, season to taste and allow to cool.

Cut the mozzarella into 16 equal cubes, about 2cm (¾ inch) across and place a basil leaf and a sun-blush tomato on top of each. Take a handful of risotto and shape into a rough ball. Make a hole in the middle with your thumb and press a piece of mozzarella inside. Cover with rice and roll into a ball on a lightly floured work surface. Repeat with the remaining ingredients.

Dip the balls in beaten egg, then roll in seasoned breadcrumbs until evenly coated. Heat some vegetable oil to 180°C (350°F) in a large pan or deep-fryer, or until a cube of bread browns in 1 minute. Deep-fry the balls, a few at a time, for 3–4 minutes until golden. Drain on kitchen paper and keep warm in a low oven while you cook the remainder.

Serve the arancini on a bitter salad of chicory and radicchio, dressed with a balsamic vinaigrette and a few thin slices of grapefruit.

Ripe and ready for the cheeseboard

RIPENED SEMI-SOFT CHEESE

Creating a ripened cheese, like Camembert or Brie, requires greater attention to detail and more advanced techniques than we have covered up to this point. The delicate moulds that give these cheeses their distinctive appearance and special taste require high humidity to thrive. Our ripened cheese is a French-style cheese with a fuzzy white bloom, a creamy texture and buttery taste.

PREPARING

The mild mushroom flavour and pleasant tang of this cheese come partly from the cows' milk, but also from the growth of the mould *Penicillium candidum*, which forms its white velvety rind. This mould is available freeze-dried in sachets from dairy suppliers, and should be rehydrated the day before you make your cheese. It releases enzymes needed for flavour and successful ripening.

MAKING

Heat the milk slowly, then add the starter and mould (see page 14). Cover and keep at a constant temperature for 1–2 hours for the cultures to develop. Add the calcium chloride and rennet and leave until the curds break cleanly (see page 72). Cut the curds (see page 73) and stir gently, keeping the curds away from the sides of the pan so they don't stick. Remove some of the whey and add the salt.

SHAPING

To make one large cheese, you will need a 20cm (8 inch) mould for shaping and draining. Alternatively, you could use several small circular moulds. Choose one that is specially designed for Brie or Camembert-style cheeses as they drain easily at room temperature. Place the mould on a draining rack, ladle the curds into it and leave to drain. When the cheese is firm enough, turn it over

and leave to drain again. Keep turning every hour until it stops draining.

RIPENING

Remove the cheese from the mould and place in a ripening box (see page 75). In order to keep the humidity high, at around 85–90 per cent, try placing a damp cloth or kitchen paper in the box near the cheese. Keep the ripening box in the refrigerator and turn the cheese daily. After 6–12 days, the cheese should be almost entirely covered in mould. When it is fully covered, it is ready to be wrapped and left in the refrigerator to mature.

STORING

The cheese can be eaten after 10–12 days, but for a more intense flavour and a pungent cheese, leave it for 5 weeks or more to mature. Once opened, consume the cheese within 2 weeks.

NOW TRY: SOAKING

Once the cheese is fully ripe, it can be soaked in apple brandy or white wine to add a wonderful flavour. Seal it in a plastic container

with 100ml (3½fl oz) of apple brandy or white wine for 24 hours at room temperature, turning after 12 hours. Allow to dry, then coat in breadcrumbs and crushed hazelnuts before serving.

RIPENED SEMI-SOFT CHEESE

Makes a 20cm (8 inch) cheese

4.5 litres (7½ pints) whole cows' milk

¼ teaspoon mesophilic starter

⅛ teaspoon *Penicillium candidum*

¼ teaspoon calcium chloride, mixed with 1 tablespoon sterilized water

¼ teaspoon rennet, mixed with 1 tablespoon sterilized water

5 tablespoons salt

To make a creamy bloom cheese, follow the instructions above and overleaf.

HOW TO MAKE RIPENED SEMI-SOFT CHEESE

1

Heat the milk slowly in a water bath over a period of 20 minutes until it reaches 32°C (90°F).

2

Turn off the heat and sprinkle the starter and mould over the surface. Leave for 5 minutes, then stir in. Cover and keep warm for 1–2 hours.

5

Ladle the curds into the mould and place on a draining rack.

6

Turn the cheese after 2 hours, then every hour for 4–5 hours or until the cheese stops dripping.

Add the calcium chloride and rennet and leave for 1–2 hours until the curds break cleanly.

Cut the curds into 1–2cm (½–¾ inch) cubes, add the salt and stir gently.

Place in a ripening box in the refrigerator for 6–12 days, turning daily.

When completely covered in mould, wrap it in cheese paper and mature for 2–3 weeks.

METHOD #14

WASHED-RIND SEMI-SOFT CHEESE

There are a whole host of cheeses made in the same way as the semi-soft cheese on the previous pages, but with different types of rind. A cheese can be washed in various liquids from time to time throughout the ripening process to add flavour and colour to the rind. Famous washed-rind cheeses include Munster, Taleggio and Cabra al Vino. The liquids used to wash these cheeses include cider, beer, strong spirits, whey and buttermilk and each creates a different taste. We use a local marmalade vodka to complement the tang of our ripened goats' cheese. Infused spirits are potent and can balance the creamy taste of a delicate cheese.

WASHING

Two different liquids are required to wash the cheese as it ripens. One is the vodka, the other is a bacterial solution, made by mixing some *Penicillium candidum* culture with salt and sterilized water. You will need to mix a fresh batch of bacterial solution each time you need it as it does not keep. Wash the cheese twice a week, alternating between the two different liquids. Pour a little bit of the liquid into a small bowl, dip in a small piece of cloth and rub the surface of the cheese all over. Remove any liquid from the ripening box and return to the refrigerator.

The rind should be sticky and develop some light colour. As it ripens, the cheese will be less sticky and a decent rind should form. Consume within 3 months when you are happy with the rind and the cheese is still soft to the touch inside.

Adding colour and flavour

VODKA-WASHED GOATS' CHEESE

Makes a 200g (7oz) cheese

9 litres (15 pints) whole goats'
milk

¼ teaspoon thermophilic starter

¼ teaspoon calcium chloride, mixed
with 1 tablespoon sterilized water

½ teaspoon rennet, mixed with 1
tablespoon sterilized water

2 litres (3½ pints) saturated
brine (see page 74), chilled

250ml (8fl oz) vodka, such as
marmalade vodka

FOR THE BACTERIAL SOLUTION
250ml (8fl oz) sterilized water

¼ teaspoon *Penicillium candidum*

1 teaspoon salt

Heat the milk slowly in a water bath over a period of 20 minutes until it reaches 32°C (90°F). Turn off the heat and sprinkle the starter over the surface. Leave for 5 minutes, then stir in gently using a whisk. Cover and leave in a warm place, wrapped in a thick towel, for 1–2 hours.

Add the calcium chloride and rennet, stir in very gently with a whisk, cover again and leave for another 45 minutes.

Cut the curds into 2cm (¾ inch) cubes (see page 73) and leave to rest for 10 minutes. Stir gently with a spatula for 10 minutes before leaving to rest for 30 minutes. Then gradually raise the temperature to 38°C (100°F) over a period of 30 minutes, stirring continuously. Leave for 5–10 minutes while the curds sink.

Drain the curds in a cheesecloth-lined colander, leave for 10 minutes, then press into a cheesecloth-lined pyramid mould and place on a draining rack. Press for 1 hour with 4kg (8lb). Then unwrap, turn, wrap again and press for another 12 hours with 5kg (10lb). Repeat this process for a final 6 hours. Follow the instructions opposite and below for brining and ripening the cheese.

After pressing, soak the cheese in a saturated brine (see page 74) for 8 hours at about 10°C (50°F), then pat dry and leave at room temperature for 12 hours.

Place the cheese on a cheese mat in a ripening box (see page 75) and leave for a week at about 10°C (50°F). The humidity in the box should be about 90 per cent.

Pour 1 tablespoon of bacterial solution into a small bowl, dip a small piece of cloth into it and wash the surface of the cheese. Return to the ripening box for 3–4 days.

Wash the cheese with a little of the vodka, then continue alternating between washing with the bacterial solution and the vodka twice a week for 2 months.

Enjoy the rind — it's the tastiest part

Fried cheese is indulgent, delicious and ideal as an occasional comfort food. The nut crust makes a lovely crunchy contrast to the oozing soft centre, and the tang of the accompanying onion marmalade cuts through the creamy cheese with a bite. Make sure the frying oil is hot so the cheese doesn't absorb too much fat, and drain thoroughly on kitchen paper before serving.

SERVES 4

100g (3½oz) hazelnuts, crushed

2 small ripened semi-soft cheeses, cut into quarters

1 tablespoon plain flour

1 egg, beaten

vegetable oil, for shallow-frying

FOR THE ONION MARMALADE

2 tablespoons olive oil

4 red onions, sliced

4 garlic cloves, chopped

1 teaspoon dried chilli flakes

1 teaspoon mustard seeds

150ml (5fl oz) sherry vinegar

75ml (3fl oz) red wine

200ml (7fl oz) port

100g (3½oz) brown sugar

2-4 sprigs of fresh thyme

2 tablespoons sultanas

TO SERVE

baby beet leaf salad

thyme-flavoured bread sticks

HAZELNUT-CRUSTED CHEESE WEDGES

To make the onion marmalade, heat the olive oil in a pan over a low heat, add the onions, garlic, chilli flakes and mustard seeds and cook gently for 10–15 minutes until the onions are soft. Add the remaining ingredients and cook gently for a further 10–15 minutes until the mixture is thick and sticky.

Preheat the oven to 150°C (300°F), Gas Mark 2. Spread the crushed nuts on a baking sheet and cook in the oven for about 15 minutes, stirring from time to time, until golden.

Coat the cheese wedges in the flour, then dip in the beaten egg. Roll the cheese wedges in the nuts, turning to coat evenly. Heat some vegetable oil in a frying pan, add the cheese wedges and fry, turning occasionally, until golden on all sides. Serve on a bed of baby beet leaf salad, with bread sticks and the onion marmalade.

Molten cheese with rich flaky puff pastry and sweet, honeyed figs is utterly irresistible. Serve this sumptuous little snack with some salad leaves to soothe your guilty conscience.

SERVES 1

butter, for greasing

125g (4oz) puff pastry

plain flour, for dusting

1 tablespoon milk

1 large fresh fig

75g (3oz) ripened semi-soft cheese

1 tablespoon honey

TO SERVE

balsamic vinegar

ready-made fig glaze

a handful of rocket

FIG & CHEESE PUFFS

Preheat the oven to 180°C (350°F), Gas Mark 4, and lightly grease a baking sheet. Roll out the pastry on a lightly floured work surface to a 12–15cm (5–6 inch) square. Lightly brush with milk, then place the fig in the centre.

Cut a cross shape down into the top of the fig, not quite to the bottom, and open it out like a flower. Place the cheese in the centre and reshape the fig around it, then draw up the corners of the pastry to enclose the fig and press together to seal the parcel.

Place the parcel on the prepared baking sheet, drizzle with the honey and bake in the oven for 15–20 minutes until puffed and golden. Drizzle with a little balsamic vinegar and fig glaze and serve hot on a bed of rocket.

There are a huge array of different artisan goats' cheeses. We've chosen to recreate a French-style chèvre, ripened with a rind of white mould, using an off-the-shelf starter and attention to detail throughout the process. This creamy and slightly acidic cheese can be enjoyed before it ripens as a cream cheese, but the ripening process is well worth the effort to create that authentic taste.

MAKES 2 SMALL CHEESES

4.5 litres (7½ pints) whole goats' milk

⅛ teaspoon chèvre starter

1 teaspoon salt

RIPENED CHÈVRE

Heat the milk slowly in a water bath over a period of 15 minutes until it reaches 30°C (86°F). Turn off the heat and sprinkle the starter over the surface. Leave for 5 minutes, then stir gently for 2–3 minutes using a whisk. Cover and leave in a warm place, wrapped in a thick towel, for 6–12 hours until the pH level drops to 4.4–4.6 (see page 72).

Transfer the curds to a cheesecloth-lined colander to drain off the whey. and sprinkle with half the salt. If your cheese moulds have drainage holes, transfer the curds to the cheesecloth-lined moulds and leave for 12 hours in the refrigerator, then turn, sprinkle with the remaining salt and leave for another 12 hours to drain. Alternatively, leave in the colander in the refrigerator for 12 hours, then sprinkle with the remaining salt and transfer to the moulds for a further 12 hours.

Take the cheeses out of the moulds and leave on a cheese mat in a ripening box at room temperature for 3–5 days. When they are covered in a pale mould, transfer to a colder environment at 10°C (50°F) and leave for 2 weeks to ripen. After the allotted time, the cheese should be completely covered in a delicate white mould. Wrap in cheese paper and keep in the refrigerator for up to 2–3 weeks. Once opened, consume within 2–3 days.

METHOD #15

HARD COWS' CHEESE

Hard cows' cheeses are among the most popular cheeses in the world, and the most famous is Cheddar, made in the Cheddar Gorge in England, where it is aged in underground caves. The good news is you don't need a cave to make this at home. The farmhouse version is easy to master and you can create a mature-tasting cheese if you have the patience to wait while it ages. Many commercial hard cheeses are coloured for consistency, but we leave the colouring out as it's the taste that really matters.

PREPARING

You will need a water bath or other indirect method of heating the milk very slowly (see page 12). Don't forget to sterilize all of your equipment before you begin (see page 14).

MAKING

Heat the milk slowly, then add the starter, cover and leave to ripen. Add the rennet and stir gently for a couple of minutes, then cover and allow to rest again for 1 hour to allow the curds and whey to separate. Test the curds with your finger and when they break cleanly, cut into cubes (see page 72). Leave to rest for 20 minutes, then slowly heat the curds again, stirring gently. Turn off the heat and leave to rest for 30 minutes, then drain for 20 minutes in a cheesecloth-lined colander; the curds will re-form into a single mass during this time.

CHEDDARING

Cheddaring is the act of slicing the curds and returning to the pan to release more whey. Slice the curds into 2cm (¾ inch) thick slices on a sterilized chopping board, then return to the pan, leaving a gully in the middle where you can scoop out the whey every 15 minutes as it is released. Keep at 38°C (100°F) for 2 hours until the curds have released the whey. Turn off the heat, and then cut the curds into 2cm (¾ inch) cubes and maintain the temperature for another 45 minutes while the curds separate. Turn gently every 5 minutes, then gently incorporate the salt.

PRESSING & AGEING

Transfer the curds to a cheesecloth-lined cheese mould, about 10–12cm (4–5 inches) in diameter, packing them in tightly to avoid leaving any air pockets. Press with 5–10kg (10–20lb) for 12 hours. Unwrap, turn over and repeat 3 times.

Unwrap, sprinkle with salt and leave to stand at room temperature for several hours to dry. Wax the cheese or cover in cheesecloth (see pages 150–1) and allow to age at 8–10°C (46–50°F) for 4–6 months.

HARD COWS' CHEESE

Makes a 450g (14½oz) cheese

4 litres (7 pints) whole cows' milk
½ teaspoon mesophilic starter
½ teaspoon rennet, mixed with 1 tablespoon sterilized water
2 tablespoons salt
cheese wax (optional, see pages 150–1)

To make hard cows' cheese, follow the instructions opposite and overleaf.

WRAPPING

Once the cheese is dry after salting, you can wrap it to add flavour before ageing. Not only will an organic wrap boost the taste, it will also protect the surface of the cheese and prevent it drying out while it is ripening. The wrap can be left on if you intend to wax the cheese later.

We often wrap our cheeses in nettles as a homage to one of our favourite local cheeses. The nettles attract natural moulds and impart a delicate woodland flavour to the cheese.

You could also try the same technique with other foraged ingredients, such as wild garlic leaves for a more pungent flavour, or sorrel covering a hard goats' cheese to complement its tangy flavour.

STORING

The cheese can be stored for up to 8 months at 8–10°C (46–50°F). Once opened, consume within 2 weeks.

NETTLE-WRAPPED CHEESE

Makes 1 wrapped cheese

1 wheel of hard cheese
250g (8oz) nettle leaves

Apply the nettle wrapping after the cheese has been pressed. Freeze the nettles to remove the sting, or blanch them in boiling water for 1–2 minutes. Place the cheese on a sheet of greaseproof paper and use a pastry brush to smooth individual leaves on to the surface of the cheese in a uniform layer. When the entire cheese is covered, place in the ripening box for 1–2 months, turning once a week.

HOW TO MAKE HARD COWS' CHEESE

1

Heat the milk slowly in a water bath over a period of 20 minutes until it reaches 32°C (90°F). Turn off the heat. Sprinkle the starter over the surface. Leave for 5 minutes, then stir in using a whisk.

2

Cover and keep warm for 1 hour. Stir in the rennet and leave for another hour. When the curds break cleanly, cut into 1–2cm (½–¾ inch) cubes.

5

Cut the curds again into 2cm (¾ inch) cubes and allow to rest off the heat but in the water bath for 45 minutes. Add the salt and turn gently but don't stir vigorously.

6

Pack the curds into a cheese mould and press with 5–10kg (10–20lb) for 12 hours. Remove from the mould, unwrap, turn over, rewrap and press for 12 hours. Repeat for another 24 hours.

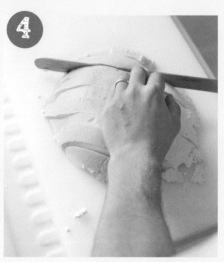

Leave for 20 minutes, then heat to 38°C (100°F) over a period of 30 minutes, stirring regularly. Maintain this temperature for another 20 minutes. Turn off the heat and leave for 30 minutes.

Transfer to a cheesecloth-lined colander and drain for 20 minutes. Cut into 2cm (¾ inch) slices. Return to the pan and keep at at 38°C (100°F) for another 2 hours.

Unwrap the cheese. Sprinkle with 1 tablespoon of salt. Leave uncovered at room temperature for 3–4 hours, then pat dry with kitchen paper. Repeat with another tablespoon of salt.

Place the cheese in a ripening box or cover in wax and age at 8–10°C (46–50°F) for 4–6 months.

Here we use this American cheese salad as a filling for a satisfying lunchtime wrap. We like using an aged hard cows' cheese in the salad, which holds its own against the other flavours, and a blue cheese in the dressing to add depth.

SERVES 4

150g (5oz) mature hard cows' cheese, diced

a handful of watercress

1 Little Gem lettuce, finely sliced

1 tomato, diced

50g (2oz) pancetta, diced and fried until crisp

100g (3½oz) cooked chicken breast, sliced

1 hard-boiled egg, chopped

1 avocado, peeled, stoned and diced

4 large soft flour tortillas

chips, to serve

FOR THE DRESSING

50g (2oz) blue cheese

1 teaspoon chopped chives

2 tablespoons white wine vinegar

1 tablespoon walnut oil

2 tablespoons olive oil

1 teaspoon lemon juice

1 teaspoon sugar

salt and freshly ground black pepper

COBB WRAPS

Make the dressing by placing all the ingredients in a food processor and blending until smooth. Season to taste.

Divide the salad ingredients between the tortillas, arranging them in a line down the centre of each. Drizzle with a little of the dressing and roll up tightly, then slice each tortilla in half at an angle. Serve with chips and the remaining dressing.

If you need a quick, tasty and colourful dish to serve to a group of hungry friends, this is an instant classic. The fresh ingredients play with the creamy melted cheese and leave your mouth with a spicy, sweet and sour sensation.

SERVES 8

200g (7oz) tortilla chips
150g (5oz) hard cows' cheese, grated
2 tablespoons soured cream
2 tablespoons Salsa (see below)
2 tablespoons Guacamole (see below)
12 slices of jalapeño pepper
a handful of fresh coriander leaves

FOR THE SALSA

3 large tomatoes, finely chopped
1 fresh red chilli, deseeded and finely chopped
1 garlic clove, finely chopped
½ a red onion, finely diced
1 tablespoon chopped fresh coriander leaves
2 tablespoons lime juice
salt and freshly ground black pepper

FOR THE GUACAMOLE

1 ripe avocado, peeled, stoned and mashed
2 tablespoons lime juice
1 tomato, finely diced
2 spring onions, finely sliced
1 garlic clove, finely chopped
1 fresh red chilli, deseeded and finely chopped
1 teaspoon chopped fresh coriander leaves

CHEESY NACHOS

To make the salsa, mix all the ingredients together in a bowl and season to taste. To make the guacamole, mix all the ingredients together in a bowl and season to taste.

To assemble the nachos, arrange one-third of the tortilla chips in a large ovenproof dish and sprinkle with one-third of the cheese. Cook under a preheated hot grill until the cheese melts, then layer another one-third of the crisps and the cheese on top and grill again to melt. Finish with the remaining crisps and cheese and grill until the cheese has completely melted and the tortillas are golden. Drizzle with the soured cream, spoon the salsa and guacamole into the centre and sprinkle the jalapeños and coriander over the top. Serve immediately.

Our hard ewes' cheese is inspired by Spanish cheeses that combine a rich creamy texture with a mellow flavour. Enjoy this as a fresh cheese, ripened for a short period of time, or leave it for up to 3 months for a more mature version.

MAKES A 450G (14½ OZ) CHEESE

9 litres (15¾ pints) whole ewes' milk

¼ teaspoon mesophilic starter

¼ teaspoon thermophilic starter

¼ teaspoon calcium chloride, mixed with 1 tablespoon sterilized water

½ teaspoon rennet, mixed with 1 tablespoon sterilized water

5 litres (8 pints) medium brine (see page 74)

HARD EWES' CHEESE

Heat the milk slowly in a water bath over a period of 15 minutes until it reaches 30°C (86°F). Turn off the heat and sprinkle the starters over the surface. Leave for 5 minutes, then stir in using a whisk. Cover and keep warm for 45 minutes.

Add the calcium chloride and stir for 1 minute to thoroughly combine, then add the rennet and stir again for 1 minute. Cover and keep warm for a further 45 minutes.

When the curds break cleanly, cut into 1cm (½ inch) cubes. Leave for 5 minutes, then stir with a large balloon whisk to cut the curds to the size of peas. Continue stirring, but now use a spatula and stir around the outside of the pan to firm up the curds and release the remaining whey.

Heat to a temperature of 40°C (104°F) over a period of 30 minutes, stirring to avoid the curds combining. Turn off the heat and leave to rest for 5 minutes. After the curds have sunk to the bottom of the pan, spoon off the surface whey until they are exposed again.

Transfer the curds to a cheesecloth-lined colander over a bucket and drain for 15 minutes. Pack the curds tightly into a cheesecloth-lined mould, about 12cm (5 inches) in diameter, and press with 5kg (10lb) for 20 minutes. Remove from the mould and unwrap. Turn over, rewrap and press again for another 20 minutes, then repeat. For the final pressing, increase the weight to 10kg (20lb) and leave overnight.

Unwrap the cheese and soak in a medium brine for 6–8 hours at 10°C (50°F) (see page 74). Pat dry and leave to ripen on a cheese mat in a ripening box at 8–10°C (46–50°F) and 80 per cent humidity. Turn over daily and leave for anything from 5 days to 3 months, wiping off any mould that appears using a piece of cheesecloth dipped in a mixture of equal weights of vinegar and salt. Once opened, store in the refrigerator and consume within 2–3 weeks.

This dish is inspired by a pesto made in the hills of Liguria in Italy, which uses broad beans instead of basil and hard ewes' cheese. If you are going to take the time to make a good cheese, you need a special pasta dish to do it justice.

SERVES 4

50g (2oz) butter

4 boneless rabbit legs, sliced

100g (3½oz) mushrooms

salt and freshly ground black pepper

50ml (2fl oz) white wine

a handful of broad bean shoots

FOR THE PESTO

75g (3oz) hard ewes' cheese, grated, plus extra to shave

150g (5oz) shelled broad beans

2 garlic cloves, peeled

12 fresh mint leaves

4-6 anchovy fillets in oil, drained

2 tablespoons lemon juice

8 tablespoons olive oil

FOR THE PASTA

250g (8oz) 00 flour, plus extra for dusting

1 egg, plus 3 egg yolks

2 tablespoons olive oil

RABBIT & BROAD BEAN PASTA

To make the pasta, place all the ingredients in a food processor, add a pinch of salt and blend until it comes together into a dough. Transfer to a lightly floured work surface and knead for 10 minutes, then place in a bowl, cover with a cloth and leave to rest for 30 minutes.

To make the pesto, place all the ingredients in a food processor, season to taste and blend until smooth. Alternatively, use a pestle and mortar to reduce the ingredients to a paste. If you prefer a sweeter pesto, blanch the broad beans in a pan of lightly salted water for 1–2 minutes, then slip off the skins before adding the beans to the pesto.

Roll the pasta dough to 1mm (¹⁄₁₆ inch) thick using a rolling pin or a pasta machine. Tear into 10cm (4 inch) squares and dust with flour to prevent them sticking together.

Melt the butter in a frying pan over a high heat, add the rabbit and mushrooms, season to taste and cook for 3–5 minutes until golden. Add the wine and cook until almost completely reduced, then remove from the heat and stir in the pesto.

Meanwhile, cook the pasta squares, a few at a time, in a large pan of lightly salted boiling water for 3 minutes, then toss with the sauce along with 2 tablespoons of the pasta cooking liquid. Mix well, divide between 4 bowls and serve topped with some bean shoots and hard ewes' cheese shavings.

This tangy goats' cheese is delicious and worth taking the time to make. It is extremely versatile - superb in salads, sliced on toast or marinaded in olive oil with pink peppercorns and fennel seeds.

MAKES 750G (1½ LB)

9 litres (15¾ pints) whole goats' milk

¼ teaspoon thermophilic starter

½ teaspoon calcium chloride, mixed with 1 tablespoon sterilized water

½ teaspoon rennet, mixed with 1 tablespoon sterilized water

5 litres (8 pints) light brine (see page 74)

FIRM GOATS' CHEESE

Heat the milk slowly in a water bath over a period of 20 minutes until it reaches 32°C (90°F). Turn off the heat and sprinkle the starter over the surface. Leave for 5 minutes, then stir in using a whisk. Cover and keep warm for 30 minutes.

Add the calcium chloride and stir for 1 minute to thoroughly combine, then add the rennet and stir again for 1 minute. Cover and keep warm for a further 1 hour. When the curds break cleanly (see page 72), cut into 5mm (¼ inch) cubes. Leave for 5 minutes.

Heat to a temperature of 47°C (117°F) over a period of 45–50 minutes, stirring to avoid the curds combining. Turn off the heat and leave to rest for 30 minutes for the curds to firm.

Transfer the curds to a cheesecloth-lined colander over a bucket and drain for 5–10 minutes. Pack the curds tightly into a cheesecloth-lined mould with drainage holes, and press with 4kg (8lb) for 30 minutes. Remove from the mould and unwrap. Turn over, rewrap and press again for another 1 hour. Turn again, increase the weight to 5kg (10lb) and leave for 12 hours.

Unwrap the cheese and soak in a light brine for 12 hours at 10°C (50°F) (see page 74). Pat dry, then leave to air dry at room temperature for 2 days. Transfer to a cheese mat in a ripening box and leave to ripen at 10°C (50°F) and 65–75 per cent humidity for 2 weeks, turning over daily. Then ripen for a further 2–3 months, turning weekly for the first month and wiping off any mould that appears using a piece of cheesecloth dipped in a mixture of equal weights of vinegar and salt.

Once opened, store the cheese in the refrigerator and consume within 1–2 months.

This dish celebrates the firm goats' cheese by adding a brioche crumb, a drizzle of fragrant local honey and an accompaniment of luscious baked figs. It is rich and pure.

SERVES 4

8 fresh figs

1 tablespoon Marsala wine

2 tablespoons runny honey, plus extra for drizzling

200g (7oz) firm goats' cheese

1 tablespoon plain flour

1 egg, beaten

75g (3oz) fine brioche breadcrumbs

1 teaspoon orange zest

olive oil, for greasing

orange, fennel and toasted almond salad, to serve

honeycomb and thyme sprigs, to garnish

GOATS' CHEESE WITH BAKED FIGS

Preheat the oven to 200°C (400°F), Gas Mark 6. Place the figs on a baking tray and cut a cross shape down into the top of each, not quite to the bottom, and open them out like a flower. Drizzle the Marsala and honey over them and cook in the oven for 15–20 minutes.

Cut the cheese into 4 slices, about 1cm (½ inch) thick, and dust with the flour, shaking off the excess. Place the beaten egg in a shallow bowl, and mix the breadcrumbs and orange zest in another. Dip the cheese slices, first in the beaten egg, then in the breadcrumbs to coat evenly.

Place on a lightly greased baking tray and bake in the oven for 10 minutes, or until golden. Drizzle with a little extra honey and serve with the baked figs on an orange, fennel and toasted almond salad. Garnish with some honeycomb and thyme.

Cheese wax comes in lots of colours

WAXED CHEESE

Waxing is the way to keep your cheese from drying out and being colonized by unwanted bacteria while you age it. Traditionally, a cheese would be aged in the perfect environment, often a cave, at the ideal temperature and humidity. However, not many of us have a cave so we use waxing or cheesecloth wrapping to protect our cheeses while they age.

PREPARING

Cheese waxes are readily available from cheese-making suppliers. There are several colours available, and certain colours are traditionally used on certain cheeses. Red wax is usually used on plain Dutch-style cheeses, green on cheeses containing herbs, brown on cheeses containing peppercorns, orange on cheeses with cumin or spices, yellow or cream wax on young cheeses and black on mature cheeses that have been well aged for a harder texture. The wax is usually paraffin-based and comes in large slabs. Waxing can be used for all hard cheeses. Remove the cheese from the refrigerator 1–2 hours before you wax it, unless you plan to apply a thin coat of wax with a paintbrush before dipping.

WAXING

When you are applying wax, it is advisable to wear gloves and you may want to use disposable plates and kitchen paper to avoid mess. Don't pour the unused wax down the drain and, if you spill any, wait until it hardens and scrape it off with a blunt knife.

The first optional stage of waxing is to paint a thin layer of wax over the surface of the cheese. This reduces the chance of small air bubbles forming on the waxed surface. If you want to have a go, place the cheese in the refrigerator overnight, then apply a coat of melted wax, about 2–4mm (just under ⅛–¼ inch) thick, to one side of the cheese using a pastry brush. Once the first side has hardened, turn the cheese over and paint the other side. Leave on a sheet of greaseproof paper to cool.

After about 2 hours, the wax will be hard enough to handle. The cheese can then be dipped in wax to create a thicker coating, following the instructions opposite. After dipping, return the cheese to the refrigerator and turn it over every day for a week to allow any moisture to evaporate.

STORING

Once waxed, a Dutch-style cheese can be aged for 3–4 months at 8–10°C (46–50°F), and a hard cows', ewes' or goats' milk cheese for 6–12 months.

NOW TRY: WRAPPING

Cheesecloth wrapping serves the same purpose as waxing but it is slightly harder to master as the wrapping does not form such an impregnable barrier as wax. For a cheesecloth wrap, start by rubbing the cheese all over with a thin layer of butter or lard. Cut 2 circles from cheesecloth, slightly larger than the top and bottom of the cheese, put them in position and rub lightly with more fat. Next cut a band of cloth long enough to go around the circumference of the cheese at least twice, put into position and rub with fat. Repeat to cover the cheese again. The cheesecloth will prevent the cheese from drying out, and is an excellent way to concentrate the flavour in a hard cheese like Cheddar.

NOW TRY: VACUUM-PACKING

If you have a home vacuum-packing machine, you can use this to extend the shelf-life of a ripened hard cheese. Semi-soft ripened cheeses can also be vacuum-packed, as long as the cheese can withstand the pressure applied by the machine. Vacuum-packing will extend the shelf-life of most cheeses by 1–2 months.

HOW TO WAX A CHEESE

Melt 50g (2oz) of wax in a bowl over a pan of lightly simmering water. Dip the bottom half of the cheese into the melted wax and hold for a few seconds.

Remove and leave the wax to harden for 1 minute before turning the cheese and dipping the other end. Allow to cool on a sheet of greaseproof paper.

Use a pastry brush to paint wax over any gaps in the wax.

The very special texture of this cheese makes it perfect for enjoying with cured meats or thinly sliced honey-glazed ham. The slightly squeaky quality evolves over time and ageing a Dutch-style cheese will give it a more mature taste and firmer consistency.

MAKES 500–750G (1–1½ LB)

9 litres (15¾ pints) whole cows' milk

¼ teaspoon mesophilic starter

¼ teaspoon calcium chloride, mixed with 1 tablespoon sterilized water

½ teaspoon rennet, mixed with 1 tablespoon sterilized water

50ml (2fl oz) water

3 litres (5¼ pints) medium brine (see page 74)

salt

about 50g (2oz) cheese wax (see page 150)

DUTCH-STYLE HARD CHEESE

Heat the milk slowly in a water bath over a period of 20 minutes until it reaches 32°C (90°F). Turn off the heat and sprinkle the starter over the surface. Leave for 5 minutes, then stir in using a whisk. Cover and keep warm for 1 hour.

Add the calcium chloride and stir for 1 minute to thoroughly combine, then add the rennet and stir again for 1 minute. Cover and keep warm for a further 1 hour. When the curds break cleanly (see page 72), cut into 1cm (½ inch) cubes. Leave for 10 minutes, then stir in 50ml (2fl oz) water at 80°C (176°F) to raise the temperature quickly. Stir for 10 minutes, then let stand for 10 minutes.

Discard 6–8 ladlefuls of whey, then replace with the same quantity of water at 65–75°C (149–167°F). The temperature should now be 38°C (100°F); maintain this temperature for 20 minutes, stirring occasionally.

Once the curds stick together, transfer to a cheesecloth-lined colander over a bucket and drain for 5 minutes. Pack the curds tightly into 3 or 4 circular cheesecloth-lined Dutch cheese moulds, about 7–10cm (3–4 inches) in diameter, and press with 500g (1lb) for 15 minutes. Remove from the moulds and unwrap. Turn over, rewrap and press again with 1–1.5kg (2–3lb) for 15 minutes. Turn again and leave overnight.

Unwrap the cheeses and soak in a medium brine for 2 hours at room temperature. Pat dry, then lightly salt the exposed tops of the cheeses and leave to air dry at room temperature for 24 hours. Wax the cheeses (see pages 150–1) and ripen at 10°C (50°F) for at least 1 month.

Once opened, store in the refrigerator and consume within 1–2 weeks.

A fondue is the cheese equivalent of a pool party. Everyone is invited and the fondue pot bubbles away like music, while guests dip in. We like to change the booze from time to time, alternating between wine, beer and cider. This is a great meal to get fussy children to eat vegetables, but don't forget to play forfeits if someone drops something in the fondue pot!

SERVES 4-6

a knob of butter

2 shallots, diced

1 garlic clove, chopped

250ml (8fl oz) dry cider

500g (1lb) Dutch-style hard cheese, grated

500g (1lb) hard cows' cheese, such as Cheddar, grated

a sprig of fresh thyme

1 heaped teaspoon smooth mustard

a pinch of grated nutmeg

salt

1 teaspoon cornflour, mixed with 1 tablespoon water (optional)

TO SERVE

chopped apples

cauliflower florets

cubes of bread

cherry tomatoes

baby pickled onions

FANTASTIC FAMILY FONDUE

Heat the butter in a pan over a low heat, add the shallots and garlic and cook gently for about 5 minutes until softened. Add the cider and bring to the boil, then reduce the heat and simmer for 10 minutes.

Meanwhile, place the grated cheese in a double boiler or a bowl over a pan of gently simmering water, add the thyme, mustard, nutmeg and salt to taste and heat very gently for 15–20 minutes until melted.

Pour the cheese and cider into a fondue pot and stir well over a low heat to mix, adding the cornflour mixture to thicken it, if necessary. Serve immediately with an assortment of chopped apples, cauliflower florets, cubes of bread, cherry tomatoes and baby pickled onions for dipping.

Jack cheese is an American classic, originally made by Mexican friars in Monterey, California. Our version contains hot peppers and is heavily influenced by its Mexican heritage.

MAKES A 12CM (5 INCH) DIAMETER CHEESE

4.5 litres (7½ pints) whole cows' milk

¼ teaspoon mesophilic starter

¼ teaspoon calcium chloride, mixed with 1 tablespoon sterilized water

¼ teaspoon rennet, mixed with 1 tablespoon sterilized water

1 tablespoon salt, plus extra for rubbing

1 tablespoon chopped fresh jalapeño peppers

1 tablespoon mixed peppercorns, crushed

1 teaspoon dried chilli flakes

JUMPIN' JACK FLASH

Heat the milk slowly in a water bath over a period of 15 minutes until it reaches 30°C (86°F). Turn off the heat and sprinkle the starter over the surface. Leave for 5 minutes, then stir in using a whisk. Cover and keep warm for 1 hour.

Add the calcium chloride and stir for 1 minute to thoroughly combine, then add the rennet and stir again for 1 minute. Cover and keep warm for a further 45 minutes.

When the curds break cleanly (see page 72), cut into 2.5cm (1 inch) cubes and leave for 5–10 minutes. Heat to a temperature of 40°C (104°F) over a period of 45 minutes, stirring continually. Turn off the heat and leave to rest for about 30 minutes until the curds mat together.

Ladle out some of the whey until you reveal the curds at the bottom, then stir for another 15 minutes until the curds hold together when squeezed in your hand.

Transfer the curds to a cheesecloth-lined colander, sprinkle with the salt, jalapeños, peppercorns and chilli flakes and drain for 5 minutes. Mix the flavouring ingredients into the cheese, then shape into a ball, draw up the corners of the cheesecloth around it and twist the top to enclose. Squeeze out the excess whey by rolling the bag of curds on a flat surface, then place on a chopping board and tie the top of the bag. Cover with a second board and press with 500g (1lb) for 6–8 hours at room temperature. The longer you leave the cheese, the firmer it will become.

Unwrap the cheese, pat dry and rub the surface with a generous layer of salt. Leave to air dry at room temperature for 24 hours, turning over once. Transfer to a cheese mat and leave to ripen in a ripening box or in the refrigerator at 10°C (50°F) for at least 2 weeks, turning over daily. Wax, wrap in cheesecloth or vacuum-pack the cheese until ready to serve.

METHOD #17

BLUE CHEESE

Blue cheese was probably first produced by mistake, but like all great discoveries it has been adapted to create something superb. We love the sheer variety of blue cheeses available and have some famous favourites, including oozy Italian Gorgonzola and crumbly tangy French Roquefort. Of course we are also biased towards British Stilton and Cornish Blue, but many regions have a blue cheese to boast about, and the blue moulds used to make the cheeses vary almost as much as their textures.

PENICILLIUM ROQUEFORTI

We make a traditional hard blue cheese with veins of mould growing inside, and a soft cheese with the blue mould forming a rind on the outside. Both use *Penicillium roqueforti* as the mould.

Mould spores are readily available in freeze-dried powder form from specialist cheese-making suppliers online. Mix the spores with sterilized water in a sterilized container and leave for 10–15 hours to rehydrate before you use it. Keep in the refrigerator and use within 3 days.

MAKING SOFT BLUE CHEESE

We use goats' milk to make a soft cheese with a blue bloom on the outside. A good growth of blue mould depends on a ready supply of oxygen. This is why we expose the cheese to the air to allow the mould to grow. Soft blue cheeses can be dusted with vegetable ash to add flavour and protect the mould as it grows. Vegetable ash can be bought online, but it is easy to make at home by wrapping 2 thinly sliced carrots and 2 thinly sliced onions in

a foil parcel and placing in the coals of a barbecue or an open wood fire until they turn to ash. You could put the parcel in a hot oven, at 200°C (400°F), Gas Mark 6, but the smoke may set off your fire alarm. When the vegetables have turned to ash, continue to heat at about 150°C (300°F) for 5–6 hours to remove any remaining moisture, then grind to a fine powder in a coffee grinder or pestle and mortar with 1 teaspoon of salt. Use a very fine sieve to dust the cheeses with a thin layer of ash. Coat the cheeses completely, then be sure to keep them at least 2.5cm (1 inch) apart in the ripening box.

MAKING HARD BLUE CHEESE

Hard blue cheese is often made with ewes' milk, but we make ours with cows' milk and add the distinctive creamy taste by combining it with double cream. The higher fat content achieved by adding cream provides the rich flavour and texture of a classic hard blue cheese.

The mould spores are sprinkled over the curds when they are packed into the cheese

SOFT BLUE CHEESE

Makes 300–400g (10–13oz)

4.5 litres (7½ pints) whole goats'
milk

⅛ teaspoon chèvre starter

⅛ teaspoon *Penicillium roqueforti*

¼ teaspoon rennet, mixed with
1 tablespoon sterilized water

1 tablespoon salt

1 tablespoon vegetable ash
(see opposite)

To make soft blue cheese, follow the
instructions opposite and overleaf.

mould, but they need oxygen to grow. We
make holes in the cheese to allow air inside,
and the mould grows in the holes and creates
the distinctive blue veins. Simply sterilize a
metal skewer and pierce the cheese in several
places from different angles. You can be as neat
or random as you like, but try to create both
vertical and horizontal holes, about 8–10 in
total. After a week or two, blue mould will
appear on the outside of the cheese, and this is a
sign of what's happening inside. Push the skewer
into the same holes again a couple of weeks later
to open them up and let in more air. Clean off
any unwanted mould that covers the outside of
the cheese using a piece of cheesecloth dipped
in vinegar.

STORING

Wrap soft blue cheese in cheese paper and
store in the refrigerator for up to 3–4 weeks
until ready to serve. The hard blue cheese
can be wrapped in foil and stored in the
refrigerator for an additional 2–4 months
until ready to serve. Once opened, consume
within 1–2 weeks.

HARD BLUE CHEESE

Makes a 500–750g (1–1½lb) cheese

2 litres (3½ pints) whole cows'
milk

2 litres (3½ pints) double cream

¼ teaspoon mesophilic starter

¼ teaspoon calcium chloride, mixed
with 1 teaspoon sterilized water

½ teaspoon rennet, mixed with
1 tablespoon sterilized water

⅛ teaspoon *Penicillium roqueforti*

1 teaspoon salt

To make hard blue cheese, follow
the instructions opposite and on
pages 162–3.

HOW TO MAKE SOFT BLUE CHEESE

Heat the milk slowly over a period of 10–15 minutes until it reaches 32°C (90°F). Turn off the heat and sprinkle the starter over the surface. Leave for 5 minutes, then stir in gently using a whisk.

Add the *Penicillium roqueforti* in the same way as you added the starter. Then add the rennet and stir again for 1 minute. Cover and keep at 32°C (90°F) for 15 hours or until the curds have formed.

Remove the cheeses from the moulds and sprinkle with salt on all sides. Leave for 10–15 minutes while the salt dissolves.

Dust the surfaces of the cheeses with vegetable ash and pat it on lightly until they are completely covered. Leave to air dry for 24 hours at room temperature.

Cut the curds into 2cm (¾ inch) thick discs and pack into 3 small cylindrical moulds, placed on cheese matting. Wait for some of the whey to drain before you fill the moulds.

Cover and leave to drain at room temperature for 24 hours, turning over every 6 hours and removing the excess whey.

Ripen the cheeses at 10°C (50°F) and 90 per cent humidity for 2 weeks. Start with the lid of the ripening box slightly ajar to control the humidity, and turn the cheeses by a quarter turn each day.

White mould should appear through the ash after 1 week, and by 2 weeks they should be completely coated. Ripen for a further 2 weeks until the ash reappears through the mould.

HOW TO MAKE HARD BLUE CHEESE

1

Heat the milk and cream slowly in a water bath over a period of 15–20 minutes until it reaches 32°C (90°F).

2

Turn off the heat and sprinkle the starter, calcium chloride and rennet over the surface. Leave for 5 minutes, then stir in using a whisk. Cover and keep warm for 2 hours.

5

Layer one-quarter of the curds into a cheesecloth-lined mould. Sprinkle with one-third of the *Penicillium roqueforti*, then repeat the layers, finishing with a layer of curds.

6

Leave to drain at room temperature for 8 hours, turning over twice. Unwrap, turn over, rewrap and leave to drain for a further 16 hours.

When the curds break cleanly, cut into 2.5cm (1 inch) cubes and leave to rest for 15 minutes. Stir gently for 1 minute, then leave to rest for another 15 minutes.

Transfer to a cheesecloth-lined colander and drain for 10 minutes, then hang up by the corners of the cloth for a further 30 minutes.

Remove the cheesecloth and sprinkle the cheese with salt. Turn over and salt the other side, then transfer to a ripening box at 10°C (50°F) and 80–90 per cent humidity for a week.

Remove excess moisture with kitchen paper, then pierce the cheese 8–10 times with a skewer. Turn over daily for 2–3 weeks, piercing again from time to time, then ripen for a further 6–8 weeks.

This is a great salad to enjoy in warm weather. The succulent melon and sharp dressing perfectly balance the rich blue cheese, the sweet ham complements its saltiness and the mint adds an extra aromatic dimension. The best part is that the whole thing takes moments to prepare.

SERVES 4-6

½ a melon, peeled and cubed

6-8 slices of air-dried ham

100g (3½oz) watercress

½ a cucumber, peeled and roughly chopped

2 sprigs of fresh mint, torn

200g (7oz) soft or hard blue cheese, crumbled

a handful of honey-roasted almonds (optional)

FOR THE DRESSING

1 tablespoon sherry vinegar

1 tablespoon olive oil

1 tablespoon walnut oil

1 teaspoon sugar

1 tablespoon lemon juice

½ teaspoon mustard

salt and freshly ground black pepper

BLUE CHEESE, MELON & MINT SALAD

Toss the melon, ham, watercress, cucumber and mint together in a large bowl and top with the crumbled cheese and almonds, if using. Whisk together the dressing ingredients in a small bowl, then drizzle over the salad just before serving so that the watercress and mint don't discolour.

Savoury galettes, made with buckwheat flour, have been a staple food in northern France for centuries. For us they are reserved for special occasions. In this recipe, we've filled our galettes with a combination of sweet pears and maple syrup, fused with salty pancetta and powerful blue cheese.

SERVES 4-6

25g (1oz) butter, melted, plus extra for greasing

150g (5oz) soft or hard blue cheese, crumbled

100g (3½oz) pear, peeled and diced

100g (3½oz) pancetta, diced and fried until crisp

2 tablespoons maple syrup

salt and freshly ground black pepper

1 teaspoon finely chopped fresh rosemary, to garnish

FOR THE BATTER

150g (5oz) buckwheat flour

50g (2oz) plain flour

2 eggs, beaten

600ml (1 pint) milk

50g (2oz) buckwheat groats, roughly ground in a coffee grinder

BLUE CHEESE GALETTES

To make the batter, whisk together the flours, eggs, milk, groats and a pinch of salt in a large bowl, cover and chill in the refrigerator for 2–4 hours.

Heat a frying pan over a medium heat, then lightly grease the pan with a piece of kitchen paper dipped in butter. Ladle about 50g (2oz)

of the batter into the pan and spread into a thin layer with the base of the ladle. Cook until golden underneath, then turn and cook the other side until golden. Remove from the pan and use the remaining batter to cook more galettes in the same way.

Preheat the oven to 200°C (400°F), Gas Mark 6, and grease a baking sheet. Prepare the parcels by sprinkling the galettes with a little cheese, pear, fried pancetta and a drizzle of maple syrup. Season with salt and pepper, then fold up and arrange on the prepared baking sheet.

Brush with melted butter and cook in the oven for 5–10 minutes until the cheese has melted inside and the galettes are crispy. Serve warm with a sprinkle of finely chopped rosemary.

be generous with your portions

METHOD #18

SERVING CHEESE

A homemade cheese that has taken so much effort deserves special treatment whether you are cooking with it or eating it fresh. Savour the moment and do it right with a cracker and a glass of wine. And never forget to take the time to choose a selection of pâtés, chutneys and fruit to accompany your creation. These 'side-kicks' are the key to enjoying your Made at Home cheese in all its splendour.

USING A CHEESE SAFE

Always bring your cheese to room temperature for at least an hour before eating it. This also makes it easier to remove the rind. We use a simple cheese safe to protect our cheese while it warms up, keeping it safe from children, pets and insects – plus hungry dinner guests. This is the perfect environment as the fly-proof mesh allows good air circulation, but prevents unwanted visitors. The only problem is that a cheese safe is a tease, and if you are hungry the temptation can prove too much.

CREATING THE PERFECT CHEESE BOARD

Laying out your cheese on a board may sound like common sense but if you want to impress your friends or family, put some thought into it. We always try to cater for different tastes and provide a variety of different colours and shapes of cheese, including at least one goats' or ewes' cheese. Cutting a few wedges or slices out of some of the cheeses will put your dinner guests at ease and a selection of oatcakes, crackers or fruity bread will provide a lovely choice.

Don't underestimate the value of accompaniments. We often provide a pot of chutney, some celery sticks, a few grapes or some squares of fruit cheese to cleanse and contrast the rich creamy cheese with something a little sharper. Finally, use a large wooden board, or a piece of slate or marble to present the cheese.

WINE PAIRINGS

There are no set rules over which cheese will go with which wine, but we tend to broadly pair certain types of cheese with certain wines, according to the table below.

CHEESE	WINE	EXAMPLES
Fresh cheeses & soft cheeses	Crisp, fruity whites or light cider	Pinot Grigio, Reisling, Chenin Blanc
Semi-soft & ripened cheeses	Aromatic whites or fruity reds	Chardonnay, Pinot Noir, Beaujolais
Hard cheeses	Red wines – the harder the cheese, the richer the grape	Merlot, Syrah, Malbec, Cabernet Sauvignon
Blue cheeses	Sweet whites and country wines	Gewürztraminer, apple brandy

TASTING CHEESE

When you have spent time making your own cheese, you will obviously be keen to eat it. We strongly believe that cheese is best enjoyed when it is served at room temperature. This develops the flavours and reinvigorates the dried curds with a degree of pliability so that you can enjoy the full depth of the cheese. If you want to draw comparisons between cheese and wine, then the terroir is certainly a factor in the making of both. Experts swear by the influence of climate, moisture and soil in wine-making and the same can certainly be said of home dairies and cheese-ripening boxes. Obviously the taste differences are less pronounced, but every single cheese in this book will taste slightly different when made in your home, than when made in ours. This is the magic of cheese and perhaps why so many artisan cheese-makers develop an obsessive fascination with the process and their individual ripening chambers.

Although we don't take it too seriously, we are still happy to try a bit of fancy cheese-tasting once in a while after dinner. To taste cheese like a connoisseur, rub a small piece between your finger and thumb to release the aroma and warm it up. Then smell the cheese with your head back to open your nasal passages. Finally eat it, allowing the creamy taste to touch different parts of your tongue. This process is purely for fun for us, but you will find that you can really taste the cheese and explore its inherent flavour.

INDEX

ACKNOWLEDGEMENTS

AUTHOR ACKNOWLEDGEMENTS

My wife Holly watched over a selection of our Made at Home cheese while she was heavily pregnant. I was away working and she was my Dairy Queen – my Miss Muffet. Thank you for all the geeky phone conversations about humidity levels, mould growth and whey. I couldn't have made this book without you. Also thanks to Brett Camborne-Paynter and Charlotte Strawbridge for helping out on the cooking days. I'd also like to thank the Octopus team for their patience and understanding at the photo shoot while Holly was in labour with our daughter Pippin, and for holding Indy while I was busy posing. Finally, thanks to cows, goats and sheep everywhere.

— *James Strawbridge*

PICTURE CREDITS

All photographs © **Nick Pope** with the exception of the following: **Monica Butnaru/Fotolia** (used throughout). **Strawbridge Family Archive** 15a, 19ar & bl, 123a & b. **iStockphoto/ Thinkstock** (used throughout).

Illustrations: **Charlotte Strawbridge** 16, 40, 54, 68.

Publisher: Stephanie Jackson
Managing Editor: Clare Churly
Copy-editor: Jo Smith
Creative Director: Jonathan Christie
Designer: Jaz Bahra
Illustrator: Charlotte Strawbridge
Photographer: Nick Pope
Stylist: Alison Clarkson
Assistant Production Manager: Caroline Alberti

MADE AT HOME
DICK & JAMES STRAWBRIDGE

CURING & SMOKING

MADE AT HOME
DICK & JAMES STRAWBRIDGE

EGGS & POULTRY

MADE AT HOME
DICK & JAMES STRAWBRIDGE

VEGETABLES

MADE AT HOME
DICK & JAMES STRAWBRIDGE

PRESERVES